Dialogue and the Development of Children's Thinking

A sociocultural approach

Neil Mercer and Karen Littleton

Routledge
Taylor & Francis Group

LONDON AND NEW YORK

First published 2007
by Routledge
2 Park Square, Milton Park, Abingdon, Oxon OX14 4RN

Simultaneously published in the USA and Canada
by Routledge
270 Madison Ave, New York, NY10016

Routledge is an imprint of the Taylor & Francis Group, an informa business

© 2007 Neil Mercer and Karen Littleton

Typeset in Times and Gill by BC Typesetting Ltd, Bristol

British Library Cataloguing in Publication Data
A catalogue record for this book is available from the British Library

Library of Congress Cataloging in Publication Data
A catalog record has been requested for this book

ISBN10: 0–415–40478–9 (hbk)
ISBN10: 0–415–40479–7 (pbk)
ISBN10: 0–203–94665–0 (ebk)

ISBN13: 978–0–415–40478–5 (hbk)
ISBN13: 978–0–415–40479–2 (pbk)
ISBN13: 978–0–203–94665–7 (ebk)

This book is dedicated to the memory of Pam Burns

Contents

Figures and tables

Figures

Tables

Preface

In any area of research, ideas develop through collective as well as individual efforts. This book is the embodiment of the 'interthinking' and collaborative work of a team of researchers, teachers and advisers who have, over 16 or so years, been committed to finding theoretically informed ways of helping children to think together. The ideas presented here have been collectively constructed by the *Thinking Together* team. The other principal members of this team have been Lyn Dawes and Rupert Wegerif, but important contributions to *Thinking Together* have also been made by Juan Manuel Fernández Cardenas, Jan English, Eunice Fisher, Jonathan Giles, Steve Higgins, Ruth Holmwood, Jenny Houssart, Judith Kleine Staarman, Tara Lovelock, Frank Monaghan, Sylvia Rojas-Drummond, Denise Rowe and Claire Sams. Pam Burns provided excellent secretarial support for the research. Many other people have also been important in shaping what we have written here, and of these we would particularly like to acknowledge the influence of Robin Alexander, Jaume Ametller, Douglas Barnes, Caroline Coffin, Mariette de Haan, Derek Edwards, Ed Elbers, Futoshi Hiruma, Paul Light, Janet Maybin, Dorothy Miell, Andy Northedge, Ingvill Rasmussen, Roger Säljo, Phil Scott, Joan Swann and Stephanie Taylor. Without the expert help of Joan Dearman and Carol Johns-Mackenzie, producing the text of this book would have been much more difficult, and excellent editorial support at Routledge has ensured that the process of publication ran smoothly. Thanks are particularly due to Lyn Dawes and Judith Kleine Staarman, who provided constructively critical comments on drafts of the manuscript, and to David Shaw, who proof-read the final version.

We wish to gratefully acknowledge the financial support for research provided by the Economic and Social Research Council (C00232236, R000232731, R000221868 and RES-000-23-0939), The Nuffield Foundation (EDU/00169/G), The Esmeé Fairbairn Foundation, Milton Keynes Council, The British Council and (in Mexico) the Consejo Nacional de Ciencia y Tecnología (CONACYT) and the Dirección General de Asuntos del Personal Académico de la Universidad Nacional Autónoma de México (DGAPA–UNAM). Our thanks also go to all the teachers and children who have participated in our research. (In order to maintain confidentiality, in the transcribed examples the names of all participants have been changed.)

In writing this book we have drawn on our body of previously published research and teaching materials. Some of the material in Chapter 7 is also included in an article by Neil Mercer entitled, 'The seeds of time: Why classroom dialogue needs a temporal analysis', in the *Journal of Learning Sciences*, volume 16.

Figure 2.1 is reprinted with permission from Taylor and Francis. This figure originally appeared in D. Faulkner, K. Littleton and M. Woodhead (1998) *Learning Relationships in the Classroom*, London: Routledge.

Figure 4.1 is reproduced with the kind permission of Phil Scott.

Appendix A is reprinted with permission from Taylor and Francis. The material originally appeared in L. Dawes and C. Sams (2004) *Talk Box: Speaking and Listening Activities for Learning at Key Stage 1*, London: David Fulton.

Notes on transcription

We have used a very simple transcription format, in which speech is rendered as grammatical phrases and sentences, to represent the sense that we, as researchers with access to the raw data, made of what was said. Information about equipment, non-verbal aspects of communication and any other contextual information that we considered pertinent to the analysis is to be found in italics in a third column or in parentheses. Our judgement was that the inclusion of additional information at our disposal, such as length of pauses or other prosodic and contextual details, would be distracting to readers and irrelevant to the issues we are addressing. Non-word utterances such as 'mm'/'ooh' are included when they are judged to have a communicative function (for example to show surprise, agreement, or to extend a speaker's turn in the face of possible interruptions). Words spoken emphatically are in italics. Simultaneous speech is shown by the use of brackets ([ ) preceding each utterance. Where the accurate transcription of a word is in doubt, it is in parentheses. When utterances could not be heard or deciphered, we say so.

Chapter 1

Why dialogue?

Our main aim in this book is to explain how classroom dialogue contributes to children's intellectual development and their educational attainment. To do so, we will make use of the results of research we and our colleagues have carried out in schools over the last 16 or so years, as well as the work of many other researchers. Examples drawn from interactions in classrooms will illustrate our discussion of how children develop as thinkers, problem-solvers and effective members of collective endeavours, and of how teachers contribute to that development. But we will do more than make a case for the importance of dialogue as the prime tool for helping children achieve an education from their school experience. We will also describe how talk in classrooms can be analysed in terms of its functions and quality, making clear the implications of this analysis for the practice of teaching and learning. What is now known about the psychological functions of dialogue is not only relevant to the academic study of cognitive development and learning: it is also of practical value to people such as teachers and parents who are concerned with ensuring that children are offered the best educational opportunities. Our hope is that what we have written here will inform practical action.

What kinds of dialogue are we interested in?

'Dialogue' is sometimes used in a broad sense to mean the interchange of ideas between one source and another. It is used to refer to such different processes as an individual reader grappling with the ideas in a book and negotiations between social groups or organizations. Such abstract or meta-phorical uses are not wrong or without value, but here we mean something more concrete and specific. In this book, the kind of dialogue we are inter-ested in is classroom talk. To narrow the focus even more, we will concen-trate on talk that takes place in the course of educational activities. Though we recognize the importance in educational activity of reading and writing, the use of gesture, diagrams and other non-verbal ways of interact-ing, our view is that the distinctive role of spoken language in learning and development justifies it being given attention in its own right. Moreover, although there has been a good deal of research on classroom talk, we do not think that enough attention has been given to the relationship between the quality of talk and learning outcomes. The dialogues we will consider include teacher–student exchanges and discussions amongst students. Both those types of dialogue have potential value for learning and development, but we will show that each has special functions.

Why does classroom dialogue deserve more attention?

There are many ways that people can make sense of the world together, using actions, graphic representations and various kinds of symbol systems as well as language. All of these will probably influence the ways individuals come to make sense of the world on their own. We would never claim that everything that can be thought can be thought in language, or that language is involved in all rational thinking. But language is without doubt the most ubiquitous, flexible and creative of the meaning-making tools available, and it is the one most intimately connected to the creation and pursuit of reasoned argument. Becoming an educated person necessarily involves learning some special ways of using language: and language is also a teacher's main pedagogic tool. For these reasons language, and especially spoken dialogue, deserves some special attention.

Understanding the role of spoken dialogue in learning and development must involve consideration of children as social actors, and not just as developing individuals. Social experience does not provide all children with the same language experiences, so we cannot assume that all children naturally have access to the same opportunities for developing their use of language as a tool for learning, reasoning and solving problems. This is nothing to do with the obvious differences of mother tongue, dialect and accent, which reflect children's social origins, and which tend to figure in popular debates about the quality of children's talk (and what schools should do about it). Within the social differentiation that is typical within any society today, children's language experiences may vary in other ways that, while subtle, are potentially of greater significance for their educational progress. Research in the USA has provided evidence to support the view first advanced by Bernstein (1975) and others some years ago, that the amount and quality of the dialogue children experience at home is strongly correlated with their eventual academic attainment (Hart and Risley, 1995). Although life will provide most children with a rich and varied language experience, in some homes rational debates, logical deductions, reflective analyses, extended narratives and detailed explanations may never be heard. How can children be expected to incorporate such ways of using language into their repertoires, if they have no models for doing so? Without the example and guidance of a teacher, many children may not gain access to some very useful ways of using language as a tool for reasoning, learning and working collaboratively because those 'ways with words' (Heath, 1983) are simply not part of their experience. As we will describe in Chapter 6, our own research has shown that when teachers focus on the development of children's language as a tool for reasoning, this can lead to significant improvements in the quality of children's problem solving and academic attainment. Nevertheless, relatively few schools explicitly teach this kind of language use. One of the arguments we will make in the book is that there is not enough emphasis in educational policy and practice on the value of teaching children how to use language for learning.

What do we mean by learning and development?

'Learning' and 'development' are terms that have both been used a great deal in developmental psychology, while 'learning', often in the company of 'teaching', is of course a common term in educational studies. We have used the two words together because we feel that both are required to invoke the kinds of cognitive, intellectual changes that we are interested in here. Both have been applied to individuals, to groups and to societies as a whole. The educational researcher Watkins (2003) distinguishes three influential conceptions of learning: 'Learning is being taught', 'Learning is individual sense-making', and 'Learning is building knowledge with others'. These are not at all incompatible, and from our perspective are complementary. 'Learning' is normally associated with the gaining of knowledge, with the acquisition of some fact or skill. We can learn something, and we may forget it. In this book we are not concerned with the processes by which people commit new information to memory (as when one memorizes a friend's new telephone number, or when a science student becomes able to recall the sequence of elements in the periodic table). Rather, we are concerned with the ways people learn to make sense of the world, become able to solve problems and – in school settings – take on new perspectives such as those inherent in science, mathematics and other subjects.

'Development' usually implies some change of a progressive kind. It invokes ideas of some sort of growth, the emergence of a new entity, the arrival of a new state of affairs. Children often forget something they have learned, and in many circumstances this would not be a cause for alarm; but developmental regression in a child would be expected to ring alarm bells. We are using both terms because we are not only interested in how dialogue contributes to the ways that people make sense together and gain knowledge from social interaction, but also how it enables them to become progressively more able to carry out certain kinds of intellectual activities.

How does interaction help learning and development?

Research into the processes of learning and cognitive development has been transformed in the last 20 years by the emergence of sociocultural theory, which is also sometimes described as 'socio-historical' and 'cultural-historical' (see, for example, Wertsch, 1985a; Daniels, 2001; Wells and Claxton, 2002). Its origins lie mainly in the work of the Russian psychologist Lev Vygotsky (for example, Vygotsky, 1962, 1978). Sociocultural research is not a unified field, but those within it treat communication, thinking and learning as processes shaped by culture, whereby knowledge is shared and understandings are jointly constructed. Communicative events are shaped by cultural and historical factors, and thinking, learning and development cannot be understood without taking account of the intrinsically social and communicative nature of human life.

From a sociocultural perspective, humans are seen as creatures who have a unique capacity for communication and whose lives are normally led within groups, communities and societies based on shared ways of using language, ways of thinking, social practices and tools for getting things done. Education is seen as a dialogic process, with students and teachers working within settings that reflect the values and social practices of schools as cultural institutions. A sociocultural perspective raises the possibility that educational success and failure may be explained by the quality of educational dialogue, rather than simply by considering the capability of individual students or the skill of their teachers. It encourages the investigation of the relationship between language and thinking and also of the relationship between what Vygotsky called the 'intermental' and the 'intramental' – the social and the psychological – in the processes of learning, development and intellectual endeavour. Partly through the influence of these ideas, social interaction has increasingly come to be seen as significant in shaping children's cognitive development. We give special attention to this topic in Chapter 2.

How does language enable collaborative learning?

Many human activities involve not just the sharing of information and the coordination of social interaction, but also people working together to solve problems. When they do so, people do not only interact, they 'interthink', combining their intellects in creative ways that may achieve more than the sum of the parts. In such problem-solving situations there is a dynamic engagement with ideas amongst partners, with language as the principal means for establishing shared understanding, testing out possible solutions and trying to reach some agreement. Thinking together is an important part of life, but it has traditionally been ignored or even repressed in school. In recent years, though, the potential value of children's collaborative activity for their learning and development has begun to be appreciated. In Chapter 3 we review research on children's collaborative learning for what it can tell us about the factors that contribute to joint activity being productive.

How can dialogue with a teacher help children learn?

In Chapter 4, we turn our attention to talk between teachers and students. This is a topic that has been studied by many people for many years, but new and useful insights have emerged in relatively recent times. The findings of research now offer a clearer and more secure understanding of how teacher–student dialogue can be used to good effect – and of how opportunities for productive dialogue may sometimes be squandered. Our own interest in such matters is not merely as detached observers, analysts, assessors or critics of the education system. As members of an international team of applied educational researchers, we have worked closely with teachers and children to try to understand and improve the educational process.

Discussions about the teacher's role sometimes oppose two models: the instructor and transmitter of knowledge on the one hand, and on the other the facilitator and co-learner. These models often figure in debates about the relative value of traditional and progressive educational methods, or about transferring control of education from the teacher to the learner. Such simple dichotomies are useful for political rhetoric, but are of little value for understanding what makes education more or less effective. Instead, we need to appreciate the diverse ways that the roles of teachers and learners can be enacted and to understand that they can shift and adapt within the classroom context, from one activity to another as is appropriate. As we will show, the close study of the dialogues between teachers and students can help the planning of activities to ensure that opportunities are provided for teachers and students to construct knowledge and understanding together.

What are the implications for educational theory and practice?

Vygotsky proposed that children's intellectual development is shaped by the acquisition of language, because language makes dialogue possible between children and other members of their community. This proposal is fundamental to sociocultural explanations of learning and development. But our allegiance to a sociocultural perspective does not mean that we have simply assumed the truth of Vygotsky's proposal – for which he provided little empirical evidence. One of the aims of the research we and our colleagues have carried out has been to put Vygotsky's ideas to the test. We have done so through creating and evaluating interventional educational programmes that embody a distinctive approach to language as a tool for teaching and learning. This approach, called *Thinking Together* and which is described in Chapter 5, has been tried and tested in schools in several countries. It represents sociocultural theory in action, in two rather different ways. First, it illustrates the practical consequences of basing an approach to teaching upon the notion of language as the principal cultural and psychological tool for building knowledge. Second, its implementation has allowed ordinary classrooms to become environments for testing the utility of sociocultural theory. As we will show in Chapter 6, the results have not only provided support for Vygotsky's claims about the relationship between the social and the psychological, they also have implications for educational practice.

What are the implications for future research?

A key feature of our approach to analysing and evaluating educational dialogue is to treat it as a process that is orientated to both the past and the future. That is, the meaning and value of dialogue for those involved in it depends on its history and where it is heading. This is not just a matter of the interests of speakers being brought to bear and so influencing the direction of the dialogue, but also the extent to which there is a basis of common knowledge that will enable participants to make sense together. Dialogues are cultural artefacts, because they embody participants' practical knowledge about how to talk in a particular kind of situation. Classroom dialogue depends on speakers understanding the 'rules of the game'. However, as we explain in Chapters 4, 5 and 6, those rules may not always be ones that help children gain an education from their school experience.

In any particular interaction, speakers use their existing knowledge to build contextual foundations for the progress of their talk. They use talk itself as a tool for creating new shared understanding. If we are interested in explaining and evaluating the processes of teaching and learning, we need to understand how teachers and learners use language to create new common knowledge. But this is a difficult topic to research, because spoken interaction, in classrooms or any other settings, has a temporal dimension. School lessons begin and end, but the dialogues within them do not necessarily have the same beginnings and ends. People take up topics they began to discuss on earlier occasions, refer to events that have happened in the meantime, and often orientate their discussions towards future activities and outcomes. Educational dialogues are particularly dependent on appeals to knowledge already gained and to learning goals ahead. In Chapter 7 we look at this vital, intriguing but complicated aspect of talk in classrooms and its significance for investigating and understanding learning and development.

In the final chapter of the book, we will do what is customary at that point: summarize what is known about the nature and functions of educational dialogue and draw some conclusions about how this should affect our understanding of children's learning and intellectual development. We will also draw out some implications for the practice of teaching and learning.

Chapter 2

How does interaction help learning and development?

In this book our particular interest is in how learning and development are assisted by the dialogues that take place in classrooms. We take a socio-cultural perspective and emphasize the important role of social interaction for constructing knowledge and understanding. In this chapter we present a brief review of how this topic has been defined by lines of psychological enquiry that began in the earlier part of the last century. We then go on to consider the relevance of the concepts that emerged from that research for understanding the processes of teaching, learning and cognitive development as they take place in a school environment. We also explain why we believe these concepts require some redefinition if they are to be useful for understanding education in the classroom.

The construction of understanding through action and socio-cognitive conflict

One of the most influential theorists of cognitive development has undoubtedly been Jean Piaget. Piaget began his research on the development of human understanding in the 1920s and continued his work in Switzerland on this theme for almost 60 years. 'Piaget's theory' does not, therefore, constitute a single coherent position or stance and there were notable shifts of emphasis over the years. The work for which he is best known in the English-speaking world dates from the 1940s to the 1960s. In this period, he was engaged in a form of enquiry he termed 'genetic epistemology', which involved producing an account of the nature of knowledge and intelligence in terms of its 'genesis' – its course of development. The resultant stage-by-stage account emphasized the importance of interactions between the child and the physical world. Thus at the heart of Piaget's theory is the idea that intelligence derives from the coordination of action in the child's environment. The Piagetian child can be seen almost as a solo child-scientist (Bruner, 1985) single-handedly (re)discovering physics and mathematics by grappling with the puzzles and paradoxes of the natural world. For Piaget language was: 'a system of symbols for representing the world as distinct from actions and operations that form the processes of reasoning' (Wood, 1998, p.25). Through actions, he argued, children can explore how the world works and so build personal, mental representations of it. These representations become progressively less dependent on physical experience as the mental representation becomes more sophisticated, ultimately leading to an ability to make predictions about aspects of the environment without needing to have had direct experience of them.

The development and education of the intellect were, for Piaget, a matter of the active discovery of reality. He believed that children's active construction of their own understanding is fundamental to their cognitive growth. He was deeply opposed to the idea of the transmission of knowledge from adult to child as a model for cognitive development. Interaction with adults was seen at best as irrelevant, or at worst as detrimental, interfering with children's exploration of their physical environment and hence the active construction of their understanding. He argued that what is learned is ultimately dependent on what children are able to assimilate into their emerging mental schemas, with all assimilation being a restructuring or a reinvention. 'Learning' thus refers to knowledge acquired by transmission from one person to another, as opposed to through construction (see Donaldson, 1978, p.145), and it is contrasted with the internal process of equilibration:

> Equilibration is a creative process of invention for Piaget who goes farther than almost anybody in asserting the individual construction of general logical principles. In fact he argues that direct instruction will actually inhibit the child's understandings if instruction gets in the way of the child's own exploration.
>
> (Newman *et al.*, 1989, p.92)

Learning is therefore subordinate to development in Piaget's account (Piaget, 1967). To use a horticultural analogy, he suggested that adults should largely restrict themselves to providing a rich, stimulating and generally supportive environment for children, just as a gardener provides good conditions for a plant to grow well. Just as excessive pruning, shaping or interference on the part of the gardener might well hinder the plant's development, so direct or intrusive adult intervention could be harmful to the natural trajectory of the child's intellectual development. The transmission of knowledge thereby becomes identified with a coercive social process of direct instruction. Such ideas were harnessed to support the ideology of progressive education in the UK during the 1960s and influenced the development of the curriculum:

> The stress is on how to learn, not what to teach. Running through all the work is the central notion that children must be set free to make

their own discoveries and think for themselves, and so achieve understanding, instead of learning off mysterious drills.

(Nuffield Mathematics Project, 1967, cited in Davis, 1991, p.21)

The developmental significance of interaction between peers

In contrast to his stance on instruction, and hence on the adult–child relationship, Piaget regarded interaction between children as a particularly
potent source of progress. Although not central to his main body of work,
in his early writings (most notably in 1932) he offered an argument for the
potential productivity of peer interaction in relation to cognitive development and especially in relation to the achievement of what he called 'concrete
operational' modes of thought, when children develop the ability to generate
rules based on their own experiences, in the early school years.

Piaget saw the preschool child's egocentrism – that is, their inability to
consider multiple perspectives or alternative points of view – as presenting
the major obstacle to achievement of higher level so-called operational
thinking. Operational thinking requires decentration (which is the ability
to take account of different points of view) and more generally to consider
multiple, varying factors in a given situation. According to Piaget, when
confronted with a problem to solve, preschoolers typically fix on the first
relevant factor they identify, and respond entirely in terms of that. What
the child needs, then, in order to progress is something that disturbs this
centration. Exposure to someone else who sees things differently, in a situation that calls for resolution of the conflicting responses, was seen as providing just this kind of disturbance. Crucially, Piaget considered that
inequalities of power and status were inimical to this. If children were
exposed to the viewpoint of a powerful figure such as an adult, they would
be unlikely to take issue with it. Rather, they would tend to ignore it if
possible, and comply with it if not. In the case of exposure to a differing
point of view in the context of an interaction with another child, however,
the more egalitarian social dynamics of the situation would create a pressure
towards resolution of differences. As he put it, 'Criticism is born of discussion and discussion is only possible amongst equals' (Piaget, 1932, p.409).

Even if a second child's answer is as wrong as that of the first, their
attempt to resolve their partial and centred solutions would be likely to
result in the achievement of a higher level, more decentred representation
that could embrace what was correct in both of the initial offerings. So
whereas, according to Piaget, the young child cannot treat adults' ideas on
their own merit, because of the differences in power and status involved, disagreements with other children serve to highlight alternatives to the child's
own particular point of view. Since the alternatives can be considered on
equal terms and the resulting conflicts of opinion necessitate resolution,

the children involved can be prompted towards higher level solutions, which incorporate the partial insights reflected in their initial positions. In essence, then, the germs of intellectual progress are seen in the conflict of perspectives. This account of peer facilitation of children's understanding is primarily linked to Piaget's account of the genesis of operational thinking. As we will explain in the next section, through the work of Doise and colleagues, it came to exert a substantial and wide-ranging influence.

Socio-cognitive conflict

During the 1970s and 1980s, Doise, Mugny and Perret-Clermont (for example Doise and Mugny, 1984; Perret-Clermont, 1980) conducted a series of studies investigating whether individual progress in understanding could be promoted by 'socio-cognitive conflict'. By this term they meant exposure to the conflicting ideas of peers in the context of paired or small group problem-solving. These researchers were not simply interested in whether groups of children working together would demonstrate better on-task performance than individuals; rather, the key research question was whether children who were given the opportunity to work on a task together would make greater individual progress than those who were not given such an opportunity. In order to answer this question Doise and colleagues designed studies that comprised individual pre-test and post-tests sessions, separated by a period of work on a spatial perspective-taking task undertaken either individually (in the 'control' condition) or in pairs/groups (in the 'experimental condition'). These studies used a variety of Piagetian 'concrete operations' tasks, a favourite being a 'village' task based loosely on Piaget's famous 'three mountains' task (Piaget and Inhelder, 1956). Here, model buildings were arranged on a baseboard to form a little village. The buildings were oriented in relation to a fixed mark on the baseboard, depicting, say, the village pond. The whole arrangement sat on a tabletop in front of the child. To the side of the child was another table, with an identical baseboard, but perhaps oriented differently in relation to the child. The task was to use a replica set of model buildings to recreate exactly the *same* village on this second table. The task is more or less difficult depending upon the relative orientations of the two baseboards.

Children in the experimental groups showed the most improvement in understanding, and this was explained by the researchers in terms of socio-cognitive conflict as follows. The children working in pairs or small groups would sometimes find themselves confronted with solutions that were different from their own. This conflict, and the socially engendered need to resolve it, would prompt each child to re-examine his or her own initial ideas, and could lead the children to recognize a higher order solution that resolved the conflict (Mugny *et al.*, 1981). For this to occur, it was necessary for the children's initial solutions to differ, but, surprisingly, it did not seem to be necessary for any of them to be more advanced than the others, or for any of them to be correct – just the existence of conflicting explanations seemed sufficient to stimulate more successful problem-solving. Moreover, Doise and his colleagues were able to demonstrate that simply attributing conflicting views to another child, even though that child was not physically present at all, was sufficient to bring about progress. Doise and his colleagues therefore suggested that children's mental resolution of such conflict did not necessarily occur during the session itself, during interaction, but probably happened later as a result of individual thought. In terms of understanding the productivity of interactions, then, according to this account dialogue could stimulate productive intellectual activity, but learning and development were still seen only as 'intramental', individualized processes.

Reservations about socio-cognitive conflict

Doise and his colleagues' work attracted a good deal of attention in the 1980s, and it certainly brought the role of interaction in learning into sharper focus. But their work also attracted some criticism. For example, Blaye (1988) raised doubts about the pivotal role of conflict, criticizing the concept as vague, ill-defined and hard to operationalize outside experimental research settings. Other researchers pointed to evidence that suggests that in certain circumstances peer interaction can result in regression as well as development (for example Tudge, 1989). Crucially, it seemed to some researchers that the observed benefits of collaborative activity could not be explained only in terms of the stimulation of later individual thinking, but had to involve the effects of conflict resolution through dialogue. Concepts such as 'negotiation' and 'argumentation' were used to offer a more social model of productive peer interaction (see Light and Littleton, 1999).

Whilst the notion of 'socio-cognitive conflict' remains influential, its most enduring influence on contemporary research has been to foster an interest in the socially constituted and dynamic processes through which learners negotiate and construct knowledge together: and it is that interest we will pursue here.

The co-construction of understanding

By the 1990s, many researchers began to see the need for a theory of cognitive performance that was sensitive to the:

> social and interpersonal contexts in which there are problems to solve, messages to transmit, goals to be attained, emotive challenges to overcome and past experiences that need to be remembered.
>
> (Perret-Clermont, 1993, p.198)

This concern with the social and interpersonal contexts of development led many researchers to the work of the Russian psychologist Vygotsky, whose influence on sociocultural theory we explained in Chapter 1. His work had only become understood with any clarity by researchers outside the Eastern bloc in the late twentieth century after years of suppression by the Soviet government. The broader educational relevance of his work has been well explained and discussed elsewhere (for example, see Wertsch, 1985a; Daniels, 2001), so we will not do so in any detail here. Suffice it to say that Vygotsky's writings on development and learning have come to be regarded as seminal – not only because he attempted to characterize the interpersonal interactions that take place in learning settings, but because he also sought to develop a 'cultural psychology', within which learning is seen to depend upon mediation by social, cultural and institutional processes at many levels.

Like Piaget, Vygotsky was interested in the development of cognitive processes that he termed the 'higher mental functions' – thinking, reasoning and understanding. However, whilst Piaget recognized the value of social interaction – more specifically peer interaction – for the development of thinking and reasoning, Vygotsky (1978) conceptualized social interaction as being at the core of the developmental process. Like Piaget, he described cognitive development as a constructive process, but proposed that it is not the child alone who is doing the constructing. Rather than being predominantly based on direct encounters with the physical world, for Vygotsky the construction of knowledge and understanding is an inherently social activity. Thus the child's interactions with other people, notably those who are more advanced and capable members of the society in which the child is growing up, mediate the child's encounters with the world-to-be-learned-about. The sense-making resources of society are gradually made available to the child through participating in the cultural life of the community, using artefacts, technologies and rituals in the company of others. Cognitive development is a kind of apprenticeship served by the child under the tutelage of adults whereby these 'cultural tools' become part and parcel of the child's own mental resources: a process of internalizing the knowledge gained.

The notion of a cultural tool refers not only to physical tools and artefacts but also extends to symbolic tools elaborated within a culture, so that a mathematical algorithm that allows you to do mental arithmetic is just as much a cultural tool as is a pocket calculator. Language itself, or at least any particular language, used for any particular set of purposes, can be considered the most important cultural tool. Virtually all intelligent activity involves using such cultural tools, and competence in the use of these tools is central both to intellectual development and to becoming an effective member of society. But it is important to emphasize that, in Vygotsky's view, cultural tools are not just picked up and put down as and when needed. Rather, they become part of our mental capability, affecting how we construe the world, how we approach problems and even how we relate to one another. Children 'appropriate' the tools of their culture and make them their own.

So according to Vygotsky, processes of interaction between the child and others, at the so-called *intermental* level, become the basis for processes that subsequently go on within the child – discussion, interaction and argument become internalized as the basis for *intramental* reflection and logical reasoning. Thus learning and development are seen as both interpersonal and intrapersonal processes mediated by cultural tools: mind emerges in the course of joint activity. There is a dialectical relationship between the intramental and intermental, so that the child's understanding of the world develops through interaction with others. As Vygotsky explains:

> Any function in the child's cultural development appears twice on two planes. First it appears on the social plane and then on the psychological plane. First it appears between people as an interpsychological category and then within the child as an intrapsychological category . . . internalisation transforms the process itself and changes its structure and functions. Social relations or relations among people genetically underlie all higher functions and their relationships.
>
> (Vygotsky, 1981, p.163)

The Zone of Proximal Development

The concept of a 'Zone of Proximal Development' (ZPD) is central to Vygotsky's theorizing. A child's cognitive capabilities can be defined in terms of what they can achieve unaided when faced with a task or problem. Indeed most forms of assessment involve testing what individuals can do without help. But individuals may also differ in terms of what they can achieve, or what they can understand, with help. The attainments that are possible for any child when given a measure of support and guidance are, as Vygotsky put it, within that child's ZPD. These are attainments that will be possible for that individual unaided at some point in the near future. The concept of a ZPD is thus an integral part of an *interactive* theory of cognitive development – instruction is only said to be useful when it moves ahead of development – and the ZPD can never be seen independently of the process of joint activity, it being formally defined as:

> The distance between the actual developmental level as determined by independent problem solving and the level and potential development as determined through problem solving under adult guidance or in collaboration with more capable peers.
>
> (Vygotsky, 1978, p.86)

It is interesting to note that, as with Piaget, peer interaction is flagged by Vygotsky as having a potentially important role in learning and development. But whereas Piaget's emphasis was on interactions amongst children of similar stages of development, Vygotsky's emphasis is on interactions between the more and less knowledgeable. Within this model, peer interaction can still be valuable, but would be expected to be most effective when a more competent child provides one who is less so with the kind of help that suits their ZPD. As Tharp and Gallimore (1988) put it, to the extent that peers can assist performance, learning will occur through their assistance.

'Scaffolding'

The metaphor that has been most widely used to capture the forms of guidance that support learners in their progress through the ZPD is that of 'scaffolding'. Introduced by Wood *et al.* (1976), it captures a form of 'vicarious consciousness' provided by an adult or more capable peer for the benefit of the child, referring to the ways in which the more knowledgeable partner controls:

> those elements of the task that are initially beyond the learner's capacity, thus permitting him to concentrate upon and complete only those elements that are within his range of competence.
>
> (Wood *et al.*, 1976, p.90)

It also captures the sense in which, through encouragement, focusing, demonstrations, reminders and suggestions, a learner can be supported in mastering a task or achieving understanding. To take the building analogy further, if we imagine building an arch with bricks it is easy to see the vital role played by the wooden framework used to assemble the arch. However, the role of this scaffolding is strictly temporary; when complete the arch will hold itself up, though without scaffolding it could not have been built. The adult's intellect provides a temporary support for the child's own until a new level of understanding has been achieved. Effective scaffolding reduces the scope for failure in the task while encouraging efforts to advance. Bruner writes that:

> [Scaffolding] refers to the steps taken to reduce the degrees of freedom in carrying out some task so that the child can concentrate on the difficult skill she is in the process of acquiring.
>
> (Bruner, 1978, p.19)

Scaffolding helps a learner accomplish a task they would not have been able to do on their own. But it is a special, sensitive kind of help that is intended to bring the learner closer to a state of competence that will enable them to complete the task on their own. This image is useful for highlighting the sense in which, for Vygotsky, individual self-supported competence is only possible if successful performance has been established through assisted learning.

Psychologists have attempted to study scaffolding in order to define what constitutes 'effective instruction'. For example, Wood and Middleton (1975) conducted a series of investigations of how 4-year-old children can be taught to assemble a 3D puzzle involving wooden blocks and pegs. They observed mothers' attempts to teach their own children how to complete the puzzle. The mothers who succeeded best were those who shifted their levels of intervention flexibly according to how well the child was doing. This 'contingency strategy' can be seen as a way for the mother to gauge and monitor the child's ZPD as learning proceeds, and to provide scaffolding at just the right point.

As Daniels notes, the term scaffolding could:

> be taken to infer a 'one-way' process wherein the scaffolder constructs the scaffold alone and presents it for use to the novice. [However,] . . . Newman et al. (1989) argued that the ZPD is created through negotiation between the more advanced partner and the learner, rather than through the notion of a scaffold as some kind of pre-fabricated climbing frame.
>
> (Daniels, 2001, p.59)

This emphasis on negotiation is also evident in the work of Tharp and Gallimore (1988) who extended Vygotsky's notion of the ZPD, drawing upon Wood et al.'s conception of 'scaffolding' to present what they call a theory of teaching as assisted performance. They characterize the ZPD not as a single growing point for an individual but as a multitude of 'growing edges' that relate to all areas of developing, culturally constituted competence:

> There is no single zone for each individual. For any domain of skill, a ZPD can be created. There are cultural zones as well as individual zones because there are cultural variations in the competencies that a child must acquire through interaction in a particular society. . . . Boys in Micronesia where sailing a canoe is a fundamental skill, will have a ZPD for the skills of navigation, created in interaction with sailing masters. A girl in the Navajo weaving community will experience a zone not quite like any encountered by the daughters of Philadelphia. Whatever the activity in the ZPD we find assistance is provided by the teacher, the adult, the expert, the more capable peer.
>
> (Tharp and Gallimore, 1998, p.96)

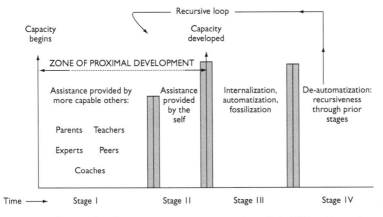

Genesis of performance capacity: progression through the ZPD and beyond

Figure 2.1 Genesis of performance capacity: progression through the ZPD and beyond.
Source: Faulkner *et al.* (1998) *Learning Relationships in the Classroom*, London: Routledge.

The development of understanding is seen as a process of guided re-invention, whereby social guidance makes it possible for the learner to achieve a constructive intellectual 're-invention' of some piece of culturally elaborated knowledge. Progression through the ZPD is described in terms of four stages, which are illustrated in Figure 2.1.

In the first stage, performance is directly assisted by more capable others through scaffolding of one kind or another. In the second, the learner effectively takes over the role of the scaffolder in relation to his or her own learning. This often means talking oneself through a task, remembering requests, reminders and injunctions previously given, and so on. The third stage is marked by the falling away of such self-guidance, as performance becomes automatic. The fourth stage just recognizes the fact that we can get thrown back to earlier stages of the acquisition process by such stressors as tiredness, or by changes in the precise conditions of the task. These stages seem to apply to the process of learning at whatever age it occurs.

What becomes evident from this brief account of Piagetian and Vygotskian perspectives is that they have many features in common. For both, learning is a matter of active construction, the ingredients for which are to be found in the physical and social world. Vygotsky's stress on the mediated character of action extends Piaget's account in ways which add to its reach in important respects, while not quarrelling with its basic tenets. In some respects the work of each might be seen as complementary to that of the other (as argued explicitly by Shayer, 2003) and certainly, between them, these two approaches to understanding development and learning have shaped almost all of the research to be described and discussed in this book.

We have gained from Piaget, Vygotsky and the researchers who have extended their work an affirmation of the value of social interaction for learning and development, whether it be interaction between learners of similar levels of understanding or between people more in the roles of learner and teacher. Both kinds of interaction will involve dialogue, enabling the effective sharing of ideas and the pursuit of some common goal. We thus reach an understanding of learning and development that transcends stark debates about whether children learn through discovery or through instruction. The available evidence supports the view that developing children are both active constructors of their own understanding and also dependent on dialogues with others to scaffold their development. The course of any child's development will depend on both their individual contribution to the dialogic process of development and that of those they interact with, in ways that will reflect the cultural tools and other knowledge resources of their communities.

Concepts such as the ZPD and scaffolding are attractive because they offer neat metaphors for the active and sensitive involvement of a teacher in students' learning. As well as being used by developmental psychologists studying parents and children in the home (for example Rogoff, 1990), the notion of scaffolding has been used in anthropological research into how craft skills (such as tailoring and weaving) are passed on from an expert to a novice in situations where the expert is often more concerned with getting the job done than with teaching (Greenfield and Lave, 1982; Lave and Wenger, 1991). In the sense Bruner and his colleagues use it, though, it represents something that seems like the essence of one kind of good teaching.

Given its attractiveness, it is not surprising that the term 'scaffolding' is now commonly used in educational research and by teachers discussing their own practice. But there is a need for caution about its being casually incorporated into the professional jargon of education and applied loosely to various kinds of support teachers provide. The essence of the concept of scaffolding as used by Bruner and colleagues is the sensitive, supportive intervention of a more expert other in the progress of a learner who is actively involved in some specific task, but who is not quite able to manage the task alone. Any other kinds of support are better described as 'help'. There is also the danger that applying the concept in the classroom depends on a simplistic comparison being made between what parents or craft experts do and what schoolteachers have to do. Schoolteachers and their students are operating under very different circumstances from parents and young children, or expert weavers and their apprentices. There is the obvious matter of teacher–learner ratios, and the more fragmented relationships that are inevitable in school. Teaching–learning interactions in classroom settings are much more complex and multifaceted:

Teachers and students interact in classrooms, they construct an ecology of social and cognitive relations in which influence between any and all parties is mutual, simultaneous and continuous. One aspect of this social and cognitive ecology is the multiparty character of the scene – many participants, all of them continually 'on-task' albeit working on different kinds of tasks, some of which may be at cross purposes. Although teachers in group discussion may attempt to enforce a participant framework of successive dyadic teacher–student exchanges, often the conversation is more complicated than that.

(Erickson, 1996, p.33)

Also, some of the definitions of scaffolding that have been used in studies of expert–apprenticeship learning and parental tutoring expressly include the criterion that the expert or the tutor is not self-consciously trying to teach, or is not primarily concerned with teaching. This clearly does not characterize the role of the professional teacher.

So where do we go from here?

A theory of teaching, learning, and cognitive development that is applicable to schools cannot be built upon comparisons with what goes on in other settings. This means that concepts like scaffolding and the Zone of Proximal Development, if they are to be of any use, have to be separated from one-to-one interactions and from the imagery of concrete physical tasks. We need to move away from parents helping infants to do puzzles, or craftworkers passing on ways of weaving cloth to apprentices. Education is not about the physical manipulation of objects, or much about individual coaching. A great deal of it is about acquiring new perspectives, new ways of representing ideas and interpreting experiences, new ways of formulating relatively abstract problems and solving them. The curriculum does not just consist of knowledge of a factual or craft-like kind, but embodies special ways of using language for handling knowledge, which students need to be enabled to understand and to use as intellectual tools. A problem with applying the concept of the Zone of Proximal Development to the school setting is that it seems to be predicated on the assessment of an individual's capabilities at one point in time, rather than with a continuing process of guided development in a collective environment.

Faced with the responsibility for the advancement of large numbers of learners, teachers have to organize, energize and maintain a local mini-community of enquiry. Teachers are expected to help their students develop ways of thinking that will enable them to travel on intellectual journeys, so that they understand and are understood in wider communities of discourse. However, teachers have to start from where the students are, to use what the students already know and help them to go back and forth across the bridge between everyday and educated ways of thinking. Within any one lesson each teacher has a diverse class of learners, each of whom has arrived with their own history, expectations and agenda (which may conflict with the teacher's agenda), and teachers can only communicate with these learners as a class, as groups, or in relatively brief individual conversations. In a primary school classroom, for example, the common patterns of communication are a teacher addressing a whole class and dipping into the activities of individuals, pairs and groups. In these ways a teacher attempts to keep all the students within the collective learning enterprise of classroom discourse, building contextual foundations for the future learning of students and creating continuity in educational activities.

If the characteristic features of school-based education are not well handled by the established, classic theories of cognitive development and learning, then what is needed is an approach to theorizing the relationship between language, learning and development that respects the complex and essentially collective nature of schooling, with its particular aims and goals and with all its inherent diversity and multiplicity. One main requirement of an educationally relevant theory, then, must be that it deals with the collective nature of the classroom. Second, it must recognize that school-based education is largely conducted through dialogues between teachers and students. Moreover, as we will go on to explain in later chapters, there is even within the constraints of the classroom a real potential for the more productive use of dialogues amongst students.

A sociocultural theory of learning and development that is applicable to the classroom must take account of the relationship between three levels of human activity: the cultural/historical, the psychological and the social/interactional:

1   *The cultural level: the collective, historical development of knowledge.* This is the level of activity of the community and society, in which schools can be recognized as culturally embedded social institutions, and so helps clarify the ways that particular cultures shape pedagogies, the goals of education and the forms of dialogue that are used to pursue them.
2   *The psychological level: individual learning and cognitive development.* More than most other approaches to learning and development, a sociocultural perspective highlights ways that activity at the cultural and social levels affects the cognitive development and learning of individuals. Sociocultural theorists certainly do not claim that intellectual development is shaped only by social, environmental factors, but they do argue that it cannot be understood without reference to the situated, social experience of the individuals in question.
3   *The social level: interaction within groups and between individuals.* This is the level of talk and dialogue. In the sociocultural model it forms a bridge between the other two levels. Through engaging in dialogue, children

encounter the culture of their community and society embodied in the language habits of this community and so discover how people around them make sense of experience. This is the level of talk as social action, and the actions people pursue through talk include those crucial to the pursuit of education – sharing information, instructing, arguing, narrating, eliciting information, assessing knowledge, demonstrating understanding and evaluating understanding.

The Intermental Development Zone

To understand how classroom education creates knowledge and guides the development of understanding (and, no less important, how it fails to do so), our theory must not only attend to how interaction is carried out at the social level (Level 3), but also be sensitive to how the forms of educational dialogue are shaped by factors at Levels 1 and 2 (i.e. cultural and psychological factors). It should account for how factors at Levels 1 and 3 affect outcomes at Level 2. We need to take account of the dynamics of classroom dialogue to achieve this, and so our theory especially needs to recognize the special role that language has in the educational process.

We have seen that within current sociocultural accounts of learning and development, the Vygotskian concept of the Zone of Proximal Development (ZPD) describes the way a child's intellectual development can reach new levels with the dialogic support of another, more knowledgeable person. But, as we explained earlier, although the ZPD implies the involvement of dialogue, it is often construed as an essentially static concept, representing the mental state of an individual learner at any one time, rather than the dynamics of development through dialogue (as Wells, 1999, p.102, also concludes). In a previous book (Mercer, 2000, Chapter 6), we introduced a different concept, the *Intermental Development Zone* (IDZ), for helping conceptualize how a teacher and a learner can stay attuned to each other's changing states of knowledge and understanding over the course of an educational activity. For a teacher to teach and a student to learn, they must use talk and joint activity to create and negotiate a shared communicative space, the IDZ, which is built from the contextual foundation of their common knowledge and aims. In the 'bubble' of this Intermental Development Zone, which is reconstituted constantly as the dialogue continues, the adult and the child negotiate their way through the activity in which they are involved. If the quality of the Zone is successfully maintained, the adult can enable a learner to operate just beyond their established capabilities, and to consolidate this experience as new ability and understanding. If the dialogue fails to keep the minds mutually attuned, the IDZ collapses and the scaffolded learning comes to a halt. The IDZ represents a continuing state of shared consciousness maintained by a teacher and learner, which is focused on the task in hand and dedicated to the objective of learning. It is represented in talk by references to shared experience, but can also be sustained by tacit invocations of common knowledge. Its quality is dependent on the contextualizing efforts of those involved. Like the notions of ZPD and 'scaffolding' (as defined by Wood *et al.*, 1976), the notion of the IDZ focuses attention on how a learner progresses under guidance in an activity; but it does so in a way that is more dynamic, more interactive and more clearly related to the task-related dialogic contributions of both teacher and learner. Vygotsky suggested that 'good' appropriate instruction could influence development. But if we say that the contribution of an adult is significant in determining what a learner achieves on any particular occasion, we must accept that this achievement is a joint one, the product of a process of interthinking. Recognizing this has profound implications for how we research cognitive development and evaluate the process of learning and teaching. For example, as well as observing the progress a learner makes with the support of a particular adult we should also observe how the adult uses language and other means of communicating to create an IDZ during the activity.

The IDZ is meant to represent a continuing event of contextualized joint activity, whose quality is dependent on the existing knowledge, capabilities and motivations of both the learner and the teacher. In this respect it fits very well the requirements of a classroom-relevant, dialogic theory. But in its original conception it too may have seemed to invoke the image of a one-to-one relationship, of a teacher and an individual student in close intellectual attunement as the student is helped to move to a new level of understanding. Is this concept applicable to the complex collectivity of the classroom, and useful if applied there? We believe that it is, if the notion of the IDZ is linked to another new concept, that of *dialogic teaching*. This idea has been developed by a classroom researcher with wide international experience, Robin Alexander, and we will consider his work in conjunction with the IDZ in some detail in Chapter 4.

The notion of intersubjectivity that is embodied in the notion of an IDZ is important. This is because through its emphasis on collectivity and dialogue it redresses the emphasis in some neo-Vygotskian research on the transmission of skills and knowledge from adult to child. Some applications of the metaphor of scaffolding arguably neglect the child's own contribution to her development – conveying an image of the child's learning as being propped up by an omniscient adult who invariably directs and controls the interaction. The allocation of such a passive role to the child oversimplifies the nature of teaching and learning interactions which are exercises in collectivity, involving both the child and the adult in processes of negotiation, disagreement, the exchange and sharing of information, judgement, decision making and evaluation of one another's contributions (Hoogsteder *et al.*, 1998). We might then use this more actively interactional conception of the teaching–learning process to conceive of a process of scaffolding that is fluid and mutually responsive, as some other educational researchers, such as Daniels, have argued is necessary:

> A rigid scaffold may appear little different from a task analysis produced by teaching which has been informed by applied behaviour analysis. A negotiated scaffold would arise in a very different form of teaching and may well be associated with collaborative activity.
>
> (Daniels, 2001, p.60)

Our attention is then directed towards:

> the creation, development and communication of meaning through the collaborative use of mediational means rather than on the transfer of skills from the more to the less capable partner.
>
> (Daniels, 2001, p.60)

In this way, our emerging theory may not only help with the analysis of teacher–student dialogue, but also help us to appreciate the educational functions of talk amongst students – which is a central topic in Chapters 5 and 6.

There is one more requirement that our emerging sociocultural theory of classroom education must satisfy: because it needs to deal with the role of dialogue in development, it must incorporate an adequate conception of the nature and functions of language. In most of what has been written in sociocultural research, the actual ways in which language functions as a cultural and social tool have not been considered in any great detail. Language has often been conceptualized rather simplistically as a single, homogeneous tool or 'mediating artefact'. A notable exception is Wells (1999), who has pointed out that language is not a single tool but rather a communicative toolkit, taking on a variety of forms and functions as it is used in the pursuit of teaching and learning.

Summary

Research has shown that interaction with adults and collaboration amongst peers can provide important opportunities for children's learning and cognitive development. The growing realization of the significance of social interaction for learning has been associated with the emerging influence of the work of Vygotsky, which has shifted the emphasis from an individualistic image of the developing child (as portrayed in the work of Piaget) towards an image of the child as growing up in a community. Concepts such as the Zone of Proximal Development, scaffolding and the Intermental Development Zone can, with some refinement, help us focus on the nature and quality of interactions in educational settings.

Chapter 3

Learning together

Chapter 2 was concerned with the role of social interaction in children's learning and development, and both adult–child interaction and that amongst children working together were discussed. In this chapter we will look in more depth at the second of these types of interaction, reviewing what research has discovered about collaborative learning. More precisely, we will be considering how knowledge and understanding can develop when learners talk and work together relatively autonomously. We will also consider what conditions are most supportive of learners' joint endeavours, so that their sessions of joint work are productive.

Whilst working and learning with other people is quite common in everyday life outside school, the history of education shows that talk amongst students has rarely been incorporated into the mainstream of classroom life. Traditionally, talk between learners in the classroom has been discouraged and treated as disruptive and subversive. Even in child-centred approaches that stress the autonomy of children, the significance of talk has tended to be downplayed in favour of individual action. Although ideas have changed to some extent in recent years, pupil–pupil talk is still regarded with unease by many teachers. As any teacher will confirm, one way that they feel their competence is judged by senior staff is: can they keep their class quiet? Of course, the reasonable explanation for the traditional discouragement of pupil–pupil talk is that, as an incidental accompaniment to whole class chalk-and-talk teaching, it is indeed disruptive and subversive. Even in less formal regimes, teachers have an understandable concern with limiting the amount of off-task talk that goes on. Thus, whilst the experience of everyday life, and the work of some researchers reviewed in the previous chapter, would seem to support the value of collaborative learning, educational practice has implicitly argued against it. So what do we really know about the educational value of students' collaboration and how relevant is this to what can, or should, happen in school?

Researching collaborative learning

Considering the role of peer interaction in learning and development compels us to be clear about what we mean when we use terms such as collaboration when referring to the processes of children's learning and joint activity.

In everyday contexts the term collaboration and cooperation are often used in very loose and general ways to indicate that people are working together to get something done. In the research literature, however, there has been considerable debate about how to define terms such as collaboration and collaborative learning (see Dillenbourg, 1999; Littleton *et al.*, 2004). We do not want to get into a lengthy and detailed discussion about definitions, but we do wish to underscore that for us collaboration means something more than children working together in a tolerant and compatible manner. When we describe children as collaborating or being engaged in collaborative learning we mean that participants are engaged in a coordinated, continuing attempt to solve a problem or in some other way construct common knowledge. Crucially, we see collaboration as involving a co-ordinated joint commitment to a shared goal, reciprocity, mutuality and the continual (re)negotiation of meaning – and this specific view of collaboration is shared by other researchers (see, for example, Barron, 2000; Nystrand, 1986). Participants in collaboration may experience what Ryder and Campell (1989) call 'groupsense' or a feeling of shared endeavour. Such coordinated activity depends upon the collaborators establishing and maintaining what Rogoff (1990) and Wertsch (1991b) have termed intersubjectivity. It will necessarily involve them in establishing a shared conception of the task or problem, and so will require the continual maintenance of intersubjectivity as they progress through the activity. Partners will not only be interacting, as they might in cooperative activity, but interthinking.

Whilst the study of children's group-based activity in school has a relatively brief history, there has been a great deal of research interest into children's collaborative working, learning and problem-solving in more general terms. It is clear from even a cursory consideration of the relevant published work that children's joint activity has been researched in diverse ways – for example, through large scale surveys of life in classrooms; experiments in which pairs or groups of children work on specially designed problem-solving tasks; and detailed analyses of talk between pairs or groups of children working on curriculum-based tasks in school. We will consider each of these in turn.

Surveying classroom activity

Perhaps one of the first messages to emerge from work surveying classroom activity is that, at least in British primary schools, truly collaborative activity rarely happens. This was the alarming conclusion of a large scale research project carried out in the 1970s called ORACLE (Galton *et al.*, 1980). The ORACLE team of researchers, observing everyday practice in a large number of British primary schools, found that just because several children were sitting together at a table (as was common) this did not mean that they were collaborating. Typically, children at any table would simply be working, in parallel, on individual tasks. While they might well have talked as they worked, and while they might possibly have talked to each other about their work, the activities they engaged in did not encourage or require them to talk and work together. This problem of children working *in* groups but rarely *as* groups has also been underscored in a number of more recent studies, some of which have shown that even when children are set joint tasks their interactions are rarely productive (Galton *et al.*, 1999; Blatchford and Kutnick, 2003; Alexander, 2004, 2005). This tells us something important about the nature of everyday educational practice and leads to the conclusion that much classroom-based talk amongst children may be of limited educational value. We will return to this issue, and what can be done about it, in Chapter 5.

Experimental studies

Much of the early collaborative learning research consisted of experimental studies of peer interaction that were designed to establish whether working and solving problems collaboratively was in fact more effective than working alone. Typically, children would be given the same task, but asked to work collaboratively or to work alone. Their performance on the task was then assessed. Reviewing such studies, Slavin (1980) noted that cooperative or collaborative learning was often judged to increase students' academic achievement, self-esteem and motivation. These sorts of investigations gave rise to a related strand of research in which independent variables, such as the size of the group (for example Fuchs and Fuchs, 2000), group composition, with respect to, for example, gender and ability (see Barbieri and Light, 1992; Howe, 1997; Webb, 1989; see also Wilkinson and Fung, 2002 for a review of work in this field), and nature of the task (for example Cohen, 1994; Light and Littleton, 1999; Underwood and Underwood, 1999) were manipulated and attempts were made to assess their effects. However, because such variables interact with each other in complex ways it has been virtually impossible to use this approach to isolate the conditions for effective collaboration. Researchers have thus started to focus less on establishing parameters for effective collaboration and more on the ways in which factors such as task design or group composition influence the nature of collaborative interaction (Dillenbourg *et al.*, 1995; Littleton, 1999; Kleine Staarman, in press). This shift to a more process-oriented kind of investigation has brought with it an interest in the talk and joint activity of learners working together on a task, with attempts being made to identify those inter-actional features that are important for learning and cognitive change.

Many experimental studies of collaborative interaction have focused on how children talk together when they are working on a problem or task. They have handled 'talk as data' by reducing those data to predefined coded categories, which in turn lend themselves to treatment by statistical analyses. In particular, correlational techniques have been used to establish whether there is evidence of an association between particular features of the learners' talk and on-task success or subsequent learning gain as indexed by individual performance on a post-test. For example, Azmitia and Mont-gomery (1993) found that the quality of children's dialogue is a significant predictor of their successful problem-solving. Studying children engaged in joint computer-based problem-solving tasks, Barbieri and Light (1992) found that measures of the amount of talk about planning, negotiation and the co-construction of knowledge by partners correlated significantly with successful problem solving by pairs, and to successful learning out-comes in subsequent related tasks by individuals. Similar analytic techniques used by Underwood and Underwood (1999) demonstrated that for pairs of children working on a computer-based problem-solving activity those who were most observed to express opinions, analyse the situation in words and express agreement and understanding achieved the best outcomes. Overall, then, the experimental evidence supports the view that focused, sustained discussion amongst children not only helps them solve problems but pro-motes the learning of the individuals involved. This conclusion may seem like common sense: but if it is so obviously true, one is led back to the ques-tion of why high quality peer discussion has not been directly promoted and facilitated in formal education.

Researching talk between pupils in the classroom

In their classic book *Communication and Learning in Small Groups*, Barnes and Todd (1977, see also 1995) show how knowledge can be treated by pupils or students as a negotiable commodity when they are enthusiastically engaged in joint tasks. They suggest that pupils are more likely to engage in open, extended discussion and argument when they are talking with their peers outside the visible control of their teacher and that this kind of talk enables them to take a more active and independent ownership of knowledge:

> Our point is that to place the responsibility in the learners' hands changes the nature of that learning by requiring them to negotiate their own criteria of relevance and truth. If schooling is to prepare young people for responsible adult life, such learning has an important

place in the repertoire of social relationships which teachers have at their disposal.

(Barnes and Todd, 1977, p.127)

Based on their detailed observations, Barnes and Todd suggest that classroom discussion has to meet certain requirements for explicitness that would not normally be required in everyday conversation. Knowledge should be made publicly accountable – relevant information should be shared effectively, opinions should be clearly explained and explanations examined critically. They also argue that the successful pursuit of educational activity through groupwork depends on learners (a) sharing a view about what is relevant to the discussion and (b) having a joint conception of what is trying to be achieved by it. These points have been supported by other research (Bennett and Dunne, 1992; Galton and Williamson, 1992) and, as you will see in Chapters 5 and 6, they are also borne out by our own work.

Barnes and Todd's ground-breaking work and approach to the study of classroom talk has influenced many other researchers investigating group interaction and joint activity. Kumpulainen and Wray (2002), for example, have provided a rich, contextually sensitive analysis of children's classroom talk using an approach they call the 'Functional Analysis of Children's Classroom Talk' (FACCT). Particular attention is paid to noting how talk can be informative, interrogative, organizational, judgemental, affective, compositional, responsive, reproductional, expositional, argumentational, imaginative, experiential, heuristic, hypothetical and intentional. They have also attempted to identify instances of talk functioning as what they call 'external thinking'. FACCT has also enabled comparisons of talk within different systems of classroom organization. An illustrative example of the kinds of issues that have emerged from this approach is provided by a case study of children's talk during a collaborative writing exercise at the computer. Summarizing their findings, Kumpulainen and Wray write:

[S]tudents did not often seem to engage in exploratory talk or participate in argumentative discourse when creating their joint text. From the point of view of the students' literacy learning, this was perhaps slightly worrying, and consideration might be paid to how to support such interaction in the course of the collaborative process in the future.

(Kumpulainen and Wray, 2002, pp.137–138)

The question of how to support children's collaborative reasoning and argumentation is one that we will return to again later in the chapter, and indeed is a theme that recurs throughout the book. But for the moment we would like to comment on another issue, highlighted by work such as Kumpulainen and Wray's. Within the research literature on collaborative learning there is considerable diversity in what is conceived of as learning and as a learning outcome. As indicated earlier, for Barbieri and Light (1992), Underwood and Underwood (1999) and others (such as Howe and Tolmie, 1999), learning is seen in terms of individual accomplishments, demonstrated through appropriate tests on individual children after group activity. Most of that research recognizes that the quality of talk and social interaction is a significant factor. However, the more radical possibility is that collaborative talk is not just a stimulant for individual thinking, but can itself be considered a social form of thinking. As some researchers have put it:

> talk and social interaction are not just the means by which people learn to think, but also how they engage in thinking. . . . [D]iscourse *is* cognition *is* discourse. . . . One is unimaginable without the other.
>
> (Resnick *et al.*, 1997, p.2)

This is a challenge to traditional, individualistic accounts of the nature of knowledge, and of learning. It implies that talk is not just the mediating means for supporting individual development, but rather that ways of thinking are embedded in ways of using language. From this perspective, the accomplishment by children of particular forms of educated discourse is a valuable educational goal in it own right. This raises the possibility, which we consider further in Chapter 5, that *how* a learner engages and interacts with other learners may have a profound and enduring impact on their attainment and, indeed, on their intellectual development.

Computers and collaboration

In recent years, with the development of new technology, interest has grown in ways that computers can support collaborative activity. Yet early visions of the place of computers in education saw the computer essentially as an individualizing technology, the perfect vehicle for delivering carefully tailored, personalized instruction, whereby each learner could be taught at their own level and pace (see Light, 1997). Advocates of children's autonomous use of computers as learning tools have tended to focus on individual activity (Papert, 1980; Gee, 2004). This may reflect the deterministic influence of the most common form of computer hardware, the 'personal computer'. Despite the constraints and affordances of the hardware, joint computer-based activity has become common in primary classrooms. Although PC screens and keyboards are not well-designed for joint use (compared with, say, interactive whiteboards), computers have the potential to resource collaborative endeavours in distinctive ways (Fitzpatrick, 1996; Järvelä, 1995; Keogh *et al.*, 2000; Wegerif and Dawes, 2004).

You may have noticed that a number of the studies of children's group-based activity we have referred to throughout this chapter, be they experimental or classroom based, have been on children's collaborations during computer-based activities. This may partly be because the situation of children working together on the computer offers researchers a nicely bounded setting in which to observe collaboration and peer interaction. But computers are also famously effective for holding children's attention! One distinctive way in which they can support collaborative learning dialogues is that they allow shared ideas to be easily represented and modified as a discussion proceeds. Talk in face-to-face dialogues exists only momentarily and only for those present. Computer-based texts offer a kind of halfway stage between the ephemerality of talk and the permanence of paper texts. As Olson (1994) has pointed out, technologies for writing and drawing can extend and deepen dialogues by turning transitory talk and thoughts into external objects that are available for critical consideration, further discussion, shared reflection and the possibility of shared reconstruction. However, the way in which teachers set up collaborative activities is crucial if computers are to provide effective support for learning dialogues between children. A computer-based activity does not exist ready-made in a piece of software; the software is just one resource for creating an educational activity.

The same software will generate significantly different activities in different classrooms, because activities are constituted through the situated interaction of the pupils, teachers and the technology. The meaning of any activity will reflect, in part, children's broader educational experiences and different classroom contexts can afford, and indeed constrain, different opportunities for learning. The established culture of learning thus impacts significantly on the collective use of computer software. So if we are to develop our understanding of the processes of productive interaction a key challenge is how to go beyond the immediate interaction between learners and particular tools and technologies to consider the cultural, institutional and historical contexts for and antecedents of groupwork. We will return to this issue in later chapters.

Supporting and promoting productive interaction

Many opportunities for collaborative learning are fortuitous. They simply emerge as a consequence of being part of a particular community of learners. That said, we still need to understand how best to enable learners' joint endeavours, so that we can promote the most effective opportunities for collaborative learning and design strategies for optimizing collaboration. This concern is reflected in some recent research, in which two factors have been given particular attention: task design, and quality of relationships.

Task design

When thinking about the issue of how to support productive group work many researchers have emphasized the significance of task design. It is important that group tasks should be designed such that learners *need* to work together on them. Therefore tasks should not be too simple, for if each child can easily solve the problem or complete the task alone, then there is no imperative for joint working. Equally, if the task is too complex for the children then they will struggle to create understanding and meaning. A group task is one that requires resources that no single individual possesses and is one in which students work interdependently and reciprocally – the exchange of ideas and information being vital to success (Cohen, 1994). It is perhaps not surprising, then, that some research suggests that open-ended, challenging tasks are more effective in facilitating productive interaction than more closed tasks focused on finding one right answer (Cohen, 1994; Van Boxtel *et al.*, 2000). This is in part because closed tasks more easily lead to one participant, perhaps a more knowledgeable person, dominating the discussion (Arvaja, 2005). A clear task structure and provision of feedback is also important and this might be one of the best ways in which computer technology can resource joint activity (Howe and Tolmie, 1999). That said, it is not simply a case of 'getting the task right'. Of course good task design helps: but because the meaning of educational tasks is created through interaction (as we argued in relation to computer-based activities), task design is only part of the story.

Quality of relationships

According to Van Oers and Hännikäinen:

> The main reason why discourses in collaborative learning processes ever lead to improved understandings is that the participants in the process are willing to share their understandings and keep on doing so *despite* their disagreements and conflicts . . . the fact that they can ever be productive at all relies on the fact that the participants in this process, for the time being, feel obliged to each other, stay with each other and maintain togetherness.
>
> (Van Oers and Hännikäinen, 2001, p.105)

This claim draws attention to the importance of the relationship between partners as they interact and work together. Researchers investigating how friendships mediate joint activity (for example Azmitia and Montgomery, 1993; Hartup, 1998; Youniss, 1999, Vass, 2003) have found that relational closeness is associated with the sharing of ideas, exchanging points of view and a collective approach to challenging tasks. It seems that the development of close relationships, characterized by a sense of trust and mutuality, enhances learning (Howes and Ritchie, 2002; Underwood and Underwood, 1999). Findings such as these have led some researchers to argue that what is needed is a 'relational' approach to group working, which properly recognizes that classroom learning is a social activity (Blatchford *et al.*, 2003). The suggestion is that training should be given to promote the development of close relationships between classmates, through amongst other things developing interpersonal trust between the children – something that is often stressed in work investigating collaborative activity in the creative arts (see Miell and Littleton, 2004). To this end, Blatchford and colleagues have developed an educational intervention programme that they characterize as using a relational approach to the development of group working. Drawing on influences from attachment theory and studies of parent–child interactions, the programme engages the participating children in activities designed to foster trust and mutual support and develop communication skills and joint problem-solving. Evaluations of the programme involving comparisons between experimental and control classes have indicated that this relational approach is not only successful in motivating children to participate in group activity and value it, but that it has a significant impact on their reading and mathematics attainment (Kutnick, 2005). As we will describe in Chapter 6, our own classroom interventions have had similar effects on group participation and academic achievement.

In the light of available evidence one cannot deny the importance of fostering positive relationships in the classroom, especially if one also considers research on the influence of gender. This issue has been studied by both experimental and observational researchers (for a review see Light and Littleton, 1999). Some of the key findings emerging from this work are neatly exemplified in the work of Swann (e.g. 1992), who has shown very clearly how the different interactive styles of boys and girls can influence the ways knowledge is constructed, and so affect the experience for those involved. Her work has drawn particular attention to the dynamics in mixed-gender groupings. Although there is a lot of individual variation amongst males and females, male students of all ages tend to dominate discussions, make more direct and directive comments to their partners, and generally adopt more executive roles in joint problem solving. A good illustration of this is her analysis of videotaped collaborative activity produced by a local education authority for the training of teachers, which compared children working in different girl–boy pairs. On the video 'successful' and 'unsuccessful' collaborations were illustrated by pairs building model cranes together from Lego with 'success' apparently being measured by design quality and sturdiness of the crane they made. But Swann points out that the 'success' of one pair was only achieved by the girl submitting to her male partner's verbal bossiness and accepting the role of his 'assistant'. In this role she had little influence on the design; her views were not taken seriously and a lot of the talk consisted of the boy giving her instructions. Swann points out that the collaboration and interaction were only being evaluated in terms of outcome, not process, with the result that some important aspects of the quality of the interaction and the nature of the educational experience for the children were being ignored.

Findings such as these illustrate that some peer-based interactions are characterized by dominance and asymmetry and such observations could be seen as adding weight to Kutnick's (2005) claim that for group activity to be effective children need to be taught to relate in positive ways.

Summary

Results from experimental studies support the view that collaboration can have a significant impact on children's learning and development. There are also good reasons for considering talk as social action – not just the means by which children learn, but also as a valuable, social mode of thinking in itself. However, observational studies have shown that collaboration in classrooms is often unproductive and inequitable. Some studies have suggested that the quality of collaboration can be improved if attention is given to developing an atmosphere of trust and mutual respect. It also seems clear that the specific design of activities, including for example the software that may be used in joint tasks, can have a significant impact. We therefore know some of the important factors associated with improving the quality of collaborative activity, but as we will explain in Chapters 4 and 5 there is more that can be done. Children have to do more than engage with each other in a positive and supportive way; they also should become able to build constructively and critically on each others' ideas. Learning to use language for reasoning is a valuable educational goal in its own right. In Chapter 5 we present the case for why we believe it is imperative to teach children how to use language to reason together, and we describe an intervention programme called *Thinking Together* designed to do this.

Chapter 4

How dialogue with a teacher helps children learn

In this chapter we examine how teachers can use dialogue to help children learn. To do so, we will draw on what is now a substantial body of findings from school-based research. Some of this we have carried out ourselves and some has been carried out by colleagues, but we will also make extensive use of the work of other researchers. The archetypal educational dialogue between a teacher and a learner is spoken, synchronous and face-to-face and it is that we will focus on here. To understand the ways that teachers and their students use spoken language in classrooms, it is important to appreciate that all kinds of dialogue, in all kinds of settings, depend on participants having some shared understanding of how to make an interaction happen. For the event to proceed smoothly, all participants must have compatible conceptions of what it is appropriate to say and do, and what it is not. These normative conceptions operate as implicit sets of rules for behaving in particular kinds of situation, which participants normally take for granted: they are 'ground rules of conversation' (Edwards and Mercer, 1987). In our early research on classroom interaction, the concept of 'ground rules' was used only in a descriptive way, to account for what we saw happening. In later research, as we will explain in due course, we began to see that these rules could be brought out into the open and examined critically not only by researchers, but by teachers and students too. In the interests of improving educational practice, they might even be changed.

Why do teachers ask questions?

In most classrooms, the world over, participants appear to implicitly accept the rule that the teacher should ask a lot of questions. One well-developed line of enquiry in educational research has been concerned with the nature and function of teachers' questions. There has been much debate amongst educational researchers over the years about the functions and value of this characteristic feature of classroom interaction (see, for example, Norman, 1992; Wells, 1999). In this debate, it was at one time very common to find researchers criticizing teachers for using questions and for talking too much. It was claimed, for example by Dillon (1988) and Wood (1992), that because most teachers' questions are designed to elicit just one brief 'right answer' (which often amounts to a reiteration of information provided earlier by the teacher) this unduly limits and suppresses students' contributions to the dialogic process of teaching-and-learning. From this point of view, teachers' frequent use of questions – especially if they are 'closed' questions, to which the teacher knows the answer – should be discouraged. There is also evidence that reducing the number of questions increases the length of children's contributions to dialogue (Wood, 1992). However, most classroom researchers would probably now agree that such judgements were too simplistic. One reason is that critics did not properly acknowledge teachers' professional responsibility for directing and assessing children's learning of a curriculum, and that it would be perverse not to rely on questions and other prompts to do so. Questions are a natural and necessary part of the teacher's linguistic toolbox, as they are for some other professions. (One might note the absence of similar criticisms of the common use of questions by general practitioners, courtroom lawyers, police interrogators, chat-show hosts, investigative journalists, helpline operators – or interviewing researchers!) Second, critics tended to assume that all question-and-answer exchanges were performing the same function. But the forms of a language do not have a simple and direct relationship to their functions. For example, we cannot assume that when someone poses a question to another person, they are always 'doing the same thing'. At an everyday level, we all appreciate this very well. In a conversation with a family member, we are likely to perceive the question 'Do you really think that you can talk to me like that?' as carrying a very different kind of message from 'Do you want a cup of tea?' Neither may be best understood as a simple request for information. The first may be essentially an expression of anger, the second an offer of a service. What is more, we all know that even an apparently simple and direct enquiry like the second one may take on special meanings within a particular relationship or setting, depending partly on the 'ground rules' as they are understood by the speakers involved.

In the classroom, teachers' questions can thus have a range of different communicative functions. For example, they can be used to test children's factual knowledge or understanding . . .

'What is the nearest planet to the sun?'

. . . for managing classroom activity . . .

'Could we have all eyes to the board please?'

. . . and as a way of finding out more about what pupils are thinking . . .

'Why did you decide to have just three characters in your play?'

Even the above account is an oversimplification, because any single question can have more than one function (for example, the third question above could be used to find out what pupils know *and* to get them to attend). Also, a question takes on a special meaning in the context of ongoing events. Compare, for example, the function of asking for the name of the nearest planet to the sun before beginning a scheme of work on the solar system, with asking the same question after it is completed. The key point is that we need to distinguish between *form* and *function* when analysing and evaluating questions in teacher–pupil dialogue: and we can only judge the function of questions, and any other forms of language, in dialogic context. While teachers' questioning certainly can require children to guess what answer is in the teacher's mind, that is merely one possible function. Teachers' questions can also serve other very useful functions in the development of children's learning and their own use of language as a tool for reasoning. They can:

- encourage children to make explicit their thoughts, reasons and knowledge and share them with the class;
- 'model' useful ways of using language that children can appropriate for use themselves, in peer group discussions and other settings (such as asking for relevant information possessed only by others, or asking 'why' questions to elicit reasons);
- provide opportunities for children to make longer contributions in which they express their current state of understanding, articulate ideas and reveal problems they are encountering.

We will go on to discuss some implications of recent research for how teachers might modify their usual ways of interacting with students: but at this point in our discussion of questions it is important to stress that we are talking about the normal, unselfconscious behaviour of many, perhaps even most, teachers in the ordinary schools where we have carried out observations. Hardly any of them have only used questions in the closed, test-like ways that critics would suggest, and all used at least some questions in a more 'guiding' way.

In order to place our discussion of questions on a more concrete basis, consider the short extract of classroom dialogue that follows (Sequence 4.1). It comes from an English primary school and in it a pair of children aged 6 to 7 are writing about mythical beasts and fairies on the computer, selecting words from a list provided on the screen. The writing they produced was intended to be read by younger children in the school. Eight pupils in the class were working on this task in pairs, and the teacher guided their activity by monitoring each pair in turn. With each pair, she would observe the current state of their progress, draw attention to certain features and use them to raise issues related to the successful completion of the activity. In the sequence below, we see the teacher making such an intervention in the activity of two girls, Carol and Lesley. (See notes on transcription in Preface.)

Sequence 4.1: Dragons

Teacher:	(*Standing behind the pair of pupils*) So what are you going to put in this one? (*points to the screen*)
Carol and Lesley:	(*muttering, inaudible*)
Teacher:	Come on, think about it.
Lesley:	A dragon?
Teacher:	A dragon. Right. Have you got some words to describe a dragon?
Carol:	[No.
Lesley:	[No.
Teacher:	(*Reading from the list on their screen and pointing to the words as she does so*) 'There is a little amazing dragon.' They could say that, couldn't they?
Carol:	[Yes.
Lesley:	[Yes.

(*Carol and Lesley continue working for a short while, with the teacher making occasional comments*)

Teacher:	Now let's pretend it's working on the computer. You press a sentence and read it out for me Lesley.
Lesley:	(*pointing to the screen as she reads*) 'Here (*pause*) is (*pause*) a (*pause*) wonderful (*pause*)'
Teacher:	Wait a minute.
Lesley:	'princess.'
Teacher:	(*turning to Carol*) Right, now you do one. You read your sentence.
Carol:	(*pointing to screen*) 'Here (*pause*) is (*pause*) a little (*pause*) princess.'
Teacher:	Good. What do you need at the end of the sentence, so that the children learn about [how
Lesley:	[Full stop.
Teacher:	Full stop. We really should have allowed some space for a full stop. I wonder if we could arrange (*pause*). When you actually draw the finished one up we'll include a full stop. You couldn't actually do it. We'll put it there. (*She writes in a full stop*) So that when you, can you remember to put

	one in? So what are the children going to learn? That a sentence starts with a?
Lesley:	Capital letter.
Teacher:	And finishes with?
Lesley:	A full stop.
Teacher:	And it's showing them? (*she moves her hand across the screen from left to right*) What else is it showing them about sentences? That you start? On the?
Lesley:	On the left.
Teacher:	And go across the page. (*She again passes her hand from left to right across the page*)

Sequence 4.1 includes some good examples of the kinds of strategies commonly used by teachers in their interactions with children. Selecting particular themes, the teacher elicits responses from the pupils that draw them along a particular line of reasoning on those themes (a line of reasoning consonant with her own goals for the activity). Moreover, she cues some of those responses heavily through the form of her questions (for example 'That a sentence starts with a . . .?'). In pursuing this line of reasoning, she has to elaborate the requirements of the activity, and in fact goes on to *redefine* those requirements (in relation to the inclusion of a full stop). She also defines the learning experience as one that is shared by her and the children through her use of 'we' and 'let's'. We can see here how a teacher uses talk, gesture and the shared experience of the piece of work in progress to draw the children's attention to salient points – the things she wishes them to do, and the things she wishes them to learn. The nature of her intervention is to remind pupils of some specific requirements of the task in hand, and so guide their activity along a path that is in accord with her predefined curriculum goals for this activity. The teacher told the researchers that she considered the activity a demanding one for the children and she was anxious that they all managed to produce some written work. We therefore interpreted her use of questions in this and other interventions we observed during this classroom activity as attempts to reduce the 'degrees of freedom' of the activity so as to ensure that its demands did not exceed the capabilities of the children and that the possible directions and outcomes of their efforts were constrained to accord with the specific goals she had set. Sequence 4.1 could thus be said to illustrate the teacher using dialogue to provide a 'scaffolding' for the children's learning (as discussed in Chapter 2) – especially as in our judgement Carol and Lesley could not have succeeded without the teacher's interventions, but did successfully complete the activity with her help. To make that judgement, we would not describe and assess the teacher's talk in an abstract, decontextualized way (by, for example, counting how many questions she used), but rather look at what questions were used for, and how well they succeeded in assisting the learning and develop-

ment of students. Our analysis would aim to be consistent with a socio-cultural perspective on teaching-and-learning as a social, situated activity.

A similar perspective on language in the classroom has been taken by Nystrand and colleagues in the USA, who have used a method they call *event history analysis* to study the antecedents and consequences of teachers' and students' questions as 'moves' in the flow of classroom discourse (for example Nystrand *et al.*, 2003). One of their special interests was in those factors that were associated with the occurrence of classroom dialogue in which students took an active and sustained part in discussing ideas, as opposed to the monologic teacher-talk that they, like so many other researchers, had observed tended to be prevalent. They called the periods of discussion in which students took an active role *dialogic spells*. Their analysis shows how teachers can break the monologic mould of classroom talk by the use of certain strategies. These include actively welcoming and soliciting students' ideas; following up students' responses in their next remarks; asking questions that do not have predetermined answers; and deliberately refraining from making the kind of evaluative feedback comment that teachers typically provide after a student's contribution (and perhaps encouraging a student to make such an evaluative follow-up instead).

How teachers can use talk to guide learning

Although the dialogues of teaching and learning must be assessed in context, generalizations can still be drawn about the relative effectiveness of certain kinds of language-based teaching strategies. For several years we have worked with colleagues in Mexico on the analysis of classroom talk, with one of our main shared interests being how teachers use language to guide children's learning. Based in schools in both the UK and Mexico, one of the aims of this research has been to improve the quality of classroom education. The Mexican strand of this research, led by Sylvia Rojas-Drummond at the National Autonomous University of Mexico (UNAM), compared teachers in state schools whose pupils had been found to develop particularly well in reading, comprehension and mathematical problem-solving, with teachers in similar schools whose pupils had not made such significant achievements. Using video recordings of classroom interactions, the research team tried to discover if the ways teachers interacted with their pupils could be related to learning outcomes. Essentially, we were trying see if some teachers were providing a more effective scaffolding for their pupils' learning. We were also interested in what kinds of learning teachers appeared to be encouraging. Our analysis covered several features of classroom interaction, including teachers' uses of questions. We looked at the content of tasks, activities and discussions, at the extent to which teachers encouraged pupils to talk together, and the kinds of explanations and instructions teachers provided to pupils for the tasks they set them.

The results of these analyses are described in more detail in Rojas-Drummond (2000), Rojas-Drummond *et al.* (2001) and Rojas-Drummond and Mercer (2004). In brief, we compared teachers in terms of the relative levels of achievement of their pupils on tests of reading comprehension and mathematics, related directly to the content of the lessons all the teachers in the study had taught. We found that the teachers whose pupils achieved the best scores could be distinguished by the following characteristics:

1   They used question-and-answer sequences not just to test knowledge, but also to guide the development of understanding. These teachers often used questions to discover the initial levels of pupils' understanding and adjusted their teaching accordingly, and used 'why' questions to get pupils to reason and reflect about what they were doing.
2   They taught not just 'subject content', but also procedures for solving problems and making sense of experience. This included teachers demonstrating the use of problem-solving strategies for children, explaining to children the meaning and purpose of classroom activities, and using their interactions with children as opportunities for encouraging children to make explicit their own thought processes.
3   They treated learning as a social, communicative process. As mentioned earlier, other research has shown that most teachers make regular use of questions. These teachers (those whose students' achievements were the highest) still did so, but compared with the other teachers they used them more for encouraging pupils to give reasons for their views, organizing interchanges of ideas and mutual support amongst pupils and generally encouraging pupils to take a more active, vocal role in classroom events.

These findings are in accord with those of other researchers, and the implications for teaching have been made clear (see, for example, Brown and Palinscar, 1989). Teachers who have been involved in this kind of research, in the UK, Mexico and elsewhere say that they have found it useful to become aware of the techniques they can use in dialogue and what can be achieved through using them. Even very good teachers, who probably do these things without being aware that they do so, nevertheless appreciate developing such meta-awareness. Yet it seems that relatively little attention has been given to these matters in the initial training and professional development of teachers.

Dialogic teaching

A useful concept that enables us to focus more precisely on the role of the teacher in classroom talk is 'dialogic teaching'. This idea has emerged from the comparative, cross-cultural research of Robin Alexander. Through his careful observations in the primary school classrooms of five countries (England, France, India, Russia and the USA), Alexander (2000) showed that if we look beneath the striking but superficial similarity of talk in class-rooms the world over, we find teachers organizing the communicative process of teaching-and-learning in very different ways. As has been noted by numerous other researchers, in most of the classrooms he observed that teachers talked more than the pupils; but the balance and nature of contribu-tions varied considerably, both between countries and between classrooms. A valuable insight provided by Alexander's research is into how the cultural contexts of schooling can shape the teachers' and students' expectations of the ways talk should be used as a tool for teaching and learning. In some ways, classroom talk sounds very similar the world over; but there seem to be some quite subtle variations in the 'ground rules' that normally apply. But he has also shown that even within countries, teachers can set up very different expectations amongst members of their class about how they should engage in dialogue. The variation he describes is not revealed by com-parisons of the extent to which teachers use questions or other kinds of verbal acts: rather, it concerns more subtle aspects of interaction such as the extent to which teachers elicit children's own ideas about the work they are engaged in, make clear to them the nature and purposes of tasks, encourage them to discuss errors and misunderstandings and engage them in extended sequences of dialogue about such matters. In some classrooms a teacher's questions (or other prompts) would elicit only brief responses from pupils, while in others they often generated much more extended and reflective talk. For example, in some of the classrooms he studied teachers encouraged children to share their misunderstandings of mathematics problems with the rest of the class, and the children responded appropriately. He explains how this can make a useful contribution not only to the development of the respondent's own understanding, but to that of their classmates too. But he found such extended dialogues were very rare.

Alexander distilled the concept of dialogic teaching from these obser-vations, drawing also on the work of the Russian scholar Bakhtin (1981). Dialogic teaching is that in which both teachers and pupils make substantial and significant contributions and through which children's thinking on a given idea or theme is helped to move forward. It is intended to highlight ways that teachers can encourage students to participate actively and so enable them to articulate, reflect upon and modify their own understanding. These ideas are interesting and provocative, and the term 'dialogic teaching' is now becoming commonly used in the educational community.

In a more recent publication Alexander (2004) suggests that dialogic teaching is indicated by certain features of classroom interaction:

- questions are structured so as to provoke thoughtful answers [. . .]
- answers provoke further questions and are seen as the building blocks of dialogue rather than its terminal point;
- individual teacher–pupil and pupil–pupil exchanges are chained into coherent lines of enquiry rather than left stranded and disconnected.

(Alexander, 2004, p.32)

Alexander's observations and recommendations resonate with our own research, as discussed earlier (Rojas-Drummond and Mercer, 2004). Dialogic teaching embodies the three characteristics that we described on page 40. There are also links with Nystrand *et al.*'s (2003) account of 'dialogic spells', Wells' (1999) 'dialogic enquiry' and Brown and Palincsar's (1989) 'reciprocal teaching'. Later in the chapter, we will show that there are also connections with recent research in science education by Mortimer and Scott (2003). There is therefore a positive convergence of research findings, with some valuable implications for classroom practice.

In terms of what the teacher actually does in classroom interaction, we can describe 'dialogic teaching' as that in which:

1   students are given opportunities and encouragement to question, state points of view, and comment on ideas and issues that arise in lessons;
2   the teacher engages in discussions with students which explore and support the development of their understanding of content;
3   the teacher takes students' contributions into account in developing the subject theme of the lesson and in devising activities that enable students to pursue their understanding themselves, through talk and other activity;
4   the teacher uses talk to provide a cumulative, continuing, contextual frame to enable students' involvement with the new knowledge they are encountering.

The final point in this list allows a useful link to be made between dialogic teaching and a concept we introduced in Chapter 2: *the Intermental Development Zone* (IDZ). The IDZ is a cumulative, goal-orientated, dynamic, contextual knowledge framework. The notion of minds being attuned in the pursuit of a common task is easiest to imagine if there are only two people involved: but one of the characteristics of the effective teacher, as Alexander argues, is that they are able to carry the attention and developing understanding of many, if not all, of a group or even a whole class along with them. The 'dialogic teacher' will use a range of discursive strategies, as appropriate, to establish and maintain a collective IDZ.

We can illustrate some features of this kind of classroom dialogue through examples, starting with Sequence 4.2 below. It was recorded in an English primary school by a member of our research team, Juan Manuel Fernández Cardenas, who was investigating the role of computers in children's literacy development (as reported in Fernández Cardenas, 2004). In this extract, the teacher is talking with three members of her Year 5/6 class about their current activity; they are communicating by email with members of a class in another local school about a shared curriculum topic, 'How to have a healthy lifestyle'.

Sequence 4.2: Writing a message

Teacher: Right. Somebody is going to read this to me now.
Declan: 'Dear Springdale. In Science we are looking at the healthy human body. We need a lot of exercise to keep our muscles, hearts and lungs working.'
Samia: 'Working well.'
Declan: 'Working well. It also keeps our bones strong.'
Samia: Yeah. We don't need a full stop.
Teacher: Yeah. That's fine. That's all right. Carry on. 'Flies . . .'
Declan: 'Flies and other animals can spread diseases and germs. That is why it is very important to keep food stored in clean cupboards, et cetera.'
Evan: Is cupboards spelled wrong? (*It is written 'cubourds'*)
Teacher: Yes, it is spelled wrong actually. It is cup-boards. Cup-boards.
Samia: (*reading as teacher writes*) B-O-A-R-D-S.
Teacher: It's a difficult word: C-U-P cup, and then you've got the OU makes an 'ow' sound. But it's OA, boards.
Evan: O, A.
Teacher: OK. Can I ask you a question? And et cetera is ETC, not ECT. I want to ask you a question before you carry on. So why have you felt it is important as a group to send Springdale this information?
(*Several children speak together*)
Teacher: Just a minute. Let's have one answer at a time.
Samia: Cause if they haven't done it yet. We can give them the information
Teacher: [Yeah.
Samia: [that we have found in the book and so when they do get, when they do this part they will know, they will know, so, to answer it.
Teacher: OK. Excellent. So what were you going to say Declan?
Declan: So they can have a healthy body and they can use it for information.
Teacher: OK.
Evan: And plus, if they haven't got the books.
Teacher: And if they haven't got the books. Now before you tell me anything else you've found in a book, I think, don't know what you think, do you think it would be a good idea to tell them

	why you are, what you've just explained to me? We are sending you this information because?
Samia:	Just because, we couldn't find, something like (*pause*)
Declan:	They could be doing it right now.
Teacher:	Well, they might be.
Samia:	We are sending you this piece of information just in case you haven't done it yet, to help you.
Teacher:	Right, discuss it how you want to say that. OK?

In the first part of Sequence 4.2, the teacher uses prompts to learn what the children have done. The first actual question comes from a child, on a point of spelling accuracy. When the teacher then begins to question the children, it is not to assess their spelling; it is to elicit their reasons for what they are writing to the children in the other school. She provides feedback on their answers ('OK. Excellent.'), so the episode has some characteristic features of classroom talk; but the teacher's questioning is used to encourage them to perceive more clearly the nature of their task. She then picks up on what they have said to guide the next part of their activity, by suggesting that it will be useful to share their reasoning with their audience (and modelling how they might do it: 'We are sending you this information because . . .'). She is using this interaction to build the knowledge foundations for the next stage of their activity – talking with them to guide their thinking forward. So we have here talk in which children make substantial and thoughtful contributions, and in which the teacher does not merely test understanding, but guides its development. What is more, all the children present are exposed to this reasoned discussion. This is not whole-class dialogue, which is the kind of talk that Alexander mainly focused on, but it clearly has characteristics of dialogic teaching.

As mentioned above, one of our interests has been in how teachers can act as models and guides for children's use of language. In a recent study of dialogue in maths teaching (reported in Mercer and Sams, 2006), we looked particularly at the extent to which teachers:

1   used 'why' questions, in which they sought children's reasons for holding an opinion, or for having carried out a particular mathematical operation;
2   used 'reasoning words' such as 'if', 'because', 'so';
3   offered reasons of their own to back up statements or proposals;
4   checked that everyone who had a relevant idea had been heard;
5   sought agreement amongst the class at the end of a debate.

To explore these ideas further, we will make some comparisons between the ways two teachers in our project schools interacted with children. Sequences 4.3 and 4.4 below show how the teachers we have called A and

B used dialogue to set up a computer-based maths activity for the children in their classes. In this activity (based on software called *Function Machine*), groups of children were asked to consider what operation had been carried out on a given number in order to end up with a second one. As well as deciding on the operation, the groups had to come up with a strategy for discovering it and for testing their ideas about it. Both sequences are taken from whole-class sessions, just before the children began to work in groups.

Sequence 4.3: Teacher A

Teacher A: OK, I'm going to make it like a bit of a quiz – something for you to think about in your groups. If you hit 'Random' the machine is going to decide on a rule for itself. Here's the machine. This is the bit where you put the numbers into the machine. The machine does some work on them and it has an output box where the numbers go to once it's done its work on them, OK? So, to put a number in you need the cursor in the input box then put a number in so. (*A child keys in '4'*) Four, thank you Amos, four it is. Now all we need to do is activate the machine. This thing lights up when you hover over it so hover over that, activate that and it has turned it into minus one. Now your job as a group is to try and think what might the machine be doing. Discuss that in your groups and when you come up with an idea, test what you think by putting some more numbers in. Has anyone got any ideas as to what the rule might be for an example? Alan? (*Alan speaks inaudibly*) Alan says it might be 'take away five', four take away five would be minus one. What does anybody else think? Well we'll try that. So we need to clear it and put some more numbers in to test it. So he says take away five. Let's put another number in so we can test it by taking away five. Two? Right, if we put two in and it is take away five, what should it be? Come in Laura, come and sit down. Minus three? Minus three, so if our rule is right, and we activate it, it will come up with minus three. That's what you are trying to do, see what the rule is, then test it with more numbers (*The teacher activates the software*) Oh! Minus *five*. Oh dear. So what would you do now? What would you have to do now in your group? You'd have to think about it again and see if you can think of another rule it might be.

Alan: It could be minus two.

Teacher A: Um – I don't think so. When you have eventually worked out what it is this box down here reveals the programme. This is quite a hard one really. This one says 'Double the input and subtract nine'. But a lot of them are a bit more one-stage operations, like add four, multiply by three, divide by two something like that. So if you get mega-mega stuck and you try it several times and you can't work it out you can have a look at it. And then think of a number you can put in and see if you can say what will come out. So we know this doubles the input and subtracts nine, so think of a number we could put in and what would come out if it's doubling the input and subtracting nine. OK? Mary?

Mary: Eighteen.

Teacher A: Eighteen. So if we put eighteen in and double the input what are two eighteens – thirty-six? And then subtract nine – what's thirty-six take away nine? (*A child responds – inaudible*) Twenty seven? – Yes twenty-seven. OK let's try it then. So if we get rid of that. I think this is going to work. Put eighteen in, activate that. Yes, twenty-seven. So once you've done that you can start all over again with a different thing. You press clear to clear it all then select 'Random' from down in this bottom corner now the machine has got a new rule in it – shall we try this one? Give me a number (*a child responds – inaudible*). Thirty-six. Oh I forgot the cursor that's why it wouldn't go in. We need the cursor – remember that. Now, thirty-six went in. Activate (*pause*) Thirteen! Thirty-six went in, thirteen came out.

Elenor: Take away three and take away twenty.

Teacher A: What might it have done? You'd be in your groups now saying what might it have done. One of you would say something and then someone would say something else, then you'd discuss it and try it.

Elenor: (*Teacher's name*) it's twenty three.

Teacher A: Well that's where I'm going to leave you to try that.

Sequence 4.4: Teacher B

Teacher B: OK. I'm going to put a number in. (*Looks at class quizzically*)

Louis: One thousand.

Teacher B: OK Louis immediately said one thousand. Is that a good number to put in?

Child: No.

Teacher B: You are shaking your head. Why do you think it is not? Shall we come back to you? You've got an idea but you can't explain it? OK Louis had one thousand. Anybody think yes or no to that idea? David.

David: Start off with an easier number.

Teacher B:	Start off with an easier number. By an easier number what kind of number do you mean?
David:	Um. Something like, lower, five.
Teacher B:	Fine. A smaller number, a lower number, yes. Louis can you see that point of view?
Louis:	Yes.
Teacher B:	If we put in a thousand we could end up with a huge number. If we put in five do you think it will be easier to work out what the machine has done?
Class:	Yes.
Teacher B:	Everyone agree?
Class:	Yes.
Teacher B:	OK, I'm going to type in five.

Teacher A essentially engages in a monologue, which runs through the procedures which the children will have to follow. The information provided is very relevant, but the event is not very interactive. The children are asked for some suggestions, but Teacher A provides few opportunities for them to do so. Questions are not used to elicit reasons, or to explore children's understanding: they are used mainly to elicit arbitrary numbers for putting into the machine. Even when the teacher appears to ask for their opinions, a response slot is not provided for them to do so; the teacher answers the question posed. (For example: 'So what would you do now? What would you have to do now in your group? You'd have to think about it again and see if you can think of another rule it might be.' And 'You'd be in your groups now saying what might it have done. One of you would say something and then someone would say something else, they you'd discuss it and try it.') No clear feedback is provided to the responses by Alan and Elenor; Teacher A does not seek the reasoning behind them, or use techniques such as reformulations to ensure that children's contributions are represented publicly and clearly in the dialogue. This teacher does not model for children the use of language for reasoning. Our classroom recordings show that Teacher A rarely provides such exemplification or guidance during whole-class sessions.

Like Teacher A, Teacher B asks questions and shares relevant information with the class about the nature of the number that is to be put into the input box of the Function Machine. But Teacher B also initiates discussion about the number by questioning the first suggestion made by a pupil, and follows this with requests for reasons for opinions and assertions. The language used in this whole-class session shows some of the common features of teacher-talk, as set out earlier: lots of questions, used for a variety of purposes. However, Teacher B uses these not simply to quiz children about their factual knowledge, or to correct their factual knowledge, but to engage them with the problem and ensure that their views are represented in the dialogue.

The teacher's contributions include 'reasoning words' such as 'what', 'how', 'if' and 'why' as the children are led through the activity. The teacher accepts and discusses the challenges made to Louis's suggestion, while respecting the contribution he made in initiating the discussion. The children are given a demonstration of how to consider the validity of alternative suggestions. Teacher B invites children to speak so that as many people as possible feel able to join in the discussion – and finally ensures that an agreement is sought and reached. In this way, through dialogue, the teacher is demonstrating to the children how effective collaboration can be an integral element of intellectual activity. None of the children makes an extended contribution to the dialogue, so it may be that this interaction does not serve as a very good example of dialogic teaching by Alexander's definition. But nevertheless the children are engaged in the discussion, their points of view are sought, they have some influence on the discussion and the actions that are taken. By being engaged in a dialogue in which talk is being used for reasoning, they are being prepared to use it when they begin their group-based activity together. Looking overall at our data from the classes of these two teachers, Teacher B's engagement with the children was certainly more 'dialogic' in both its structure and content than Teacher A's, and could be seen to more explicitly be concerned with the maintenance of the kind of dynamic, forward-looking shared frame of reference that we have called an IDZ.

Dialogic teaching in science

In recent research with Jaume Ametller, Lyn Dawes, Judith Kleine Staarman and Phil Scott, one of us (NM) has been analysing talk in science lessons in primary and secondary schools. Drawing on Scott's own previous work on science teaching (as will be explained below) as well as that of Alexander (as discussed above), the research is based on the premises that:

1   gaining scientific understanding involves taking on new conceptual frameworks and ways of evaluating knowledge;
2   the taking up of a scientific perspective quite commonly involves the critical examination of an existing 'everyday' perspective on natural phenomena;
3   this learning process consists, at least in part, of induction into a perspective and a new discourse by a relative expert (the teacher); it is not achievable by 'discovery learning' alone.

One of our aims is to describe how differences between everyday and scientific accounts are manifested in classroom talk, how they are dealt with by the teacher and what implications this has for the teaching and learning of science. We have tried to identify strategies that teachers use to engage students in constructive dialogues relating to their perspectives, assumptions and beliefs about natural phenomena and how these relate to the teaching and learning of science. Our hypothesis has been that teacher–student dialogue can mediate a shift of students' understanding of natural phenomena, from everyday to more scientific perspectives and explanations, and so our examination of classroom talk and assessment of learning outcomes has been designed to test this idea. It is hoped that this will provide new insights into the discursive processes of teaching and learning in science classrooms and how teachers can use dialogue to support student learning more effectively. We have been addressing the following research questions:

1   What is 'dialogic teaching' in a science classroom? That is, can we characterize teaching strategies that most effectively engage students in extended dialogues and assist their learning?
2   What can the analysis of classroom dialogue through a series of related lessons tell us about the ways such dialogue contributes to students' emergent understanding of specific scientific concepts or processes?
3   Do teachers of science at upper primary and lower secondary levels typically engage in different types of dialogic interaction with their students, use specific strategies, or represent scientific knowledge in different ways? Are any such differences of pedagogic significance?
4   How can the specification and exemplification of dialogic teaching contribute to educational theory and inform the professional development of teachers?

We have been studying both upper primary classes (ages 10–11) and lower secondary (ages 11–12) so as to capture some variety in the range of teachers' dialogic strategies in teaching science. The research was still ongoing at the time this book went to press; but our initial observations suggest that primary teachers are often good at sustaining dialogues with groups and individuals, and make special efforts to set up and sustain group work activities. However, they may lack confident understanding of the scientific topics being discussed and this may limit the scope of their dialogue with children. On the other hand, secondary teachers, being subject specialists, are usually more confident in dealing with scientific knowledge. They are often very skilled in holding students' attention through lively, engaging, whole class presentations – but appear to give less attention to the use of extended dialogue for assisting learning. The research is testing these impressions and so may inform the issue of how transition from primary to secondary school affects children's involvement in learning science.

In collaboration over some years, Mortimer and Scott have carefully examined the functions of dialogue in secondary science teaching (Scott, 1998; Mortimer and Scott, 2003). Their research has highlighted the problems that students often have in moving between everyday and scientific

	INTERACTIVE	NON-INTERACTIVE
AUTHORITATIVE	interactive/ authoritative	non-interactive/ authoritative
DIALOGIC	interactive/ dialogic	non-interactive/ dialogic

Figure 4.1 Four classes of communicative approach

Source: Adapted from E. F. Mortimer and P. H. Scott (2003) *Meaning Making in Science Classrooms*, Milton Keynes: Open University Press.

understandings of natural phenomena – and how dialogue with a teacher may be one means for enabling students to take a scientific perspective on natural phenomena and undertake the systematic study of them. They offer a matrix for distinguishing different types of 'communicative approach' in teacher-led talk, as shown in Figure 4.1.

They and their colleagues (Mortimer and Scott, 2003; Scott and Asoko, 2006) have explained this scheme as follows. The *interactive–non-interactive* dimension represents the extent to which the students, as well as the teacher, are actively involved in the dialogue. The *dialogic–authoritative* dimension represents the relative extent to which the students' or teacher's ideas influence the content and direction of the classroom talk. Taken together, these two dimensions allow any episode of classroom dialogue to be defined as being interactive or non-interactive on the one hand, and dialogic or authoritative on the other. Four classes of 'communicative approach' can thus be identified: interactive/dialogic, interactive/authoritative, non-interactive/dialogic and non-interactive/authoritative.

So in a interactive/dialogic episode a teacher might ask students for their ideas on a topic. The teacher might record those ideas on the board for future reference, or ask other pupils whether or not they agree with what has been said. The teacher might ask students to elaborate their ideas ('Oh, that's interesting, what do you mean by that?'). But the teacher would not make evaluations of these ideas in terms of their correctness, or lead the discussion along a narrow, pre-defined track. Classroom talk becomes more 'authoritative' when the teacher acts more explicitly as an expert, keeps to a given agenda and directs the topic of the discussion clearly along certain routes (which may reflect the structure and content of the curriculum topic being dealt with). In a non-interactive/authoritative episode the teacher would typically be presenting ideas in a 'lecturing' style.

From this scheme, Mortimer and Scott make two important points:

1 There are different types of teacher-talk, which vary in the extent to which they position the teacher as 'expert' and the extent to which they offer possibilities for substantial contributions by students.
2 These different types of talk do not represent better or worse teaching strategies in any absolute sense; the quality of the teaching depends on making the right strategic choices; and the different types of talk can function in complement.

Even in the classrooms of 'dialogic teachers' (in Alexander's sense), classroom talk need not always be 'dialogic' (in Mortimer and Scott's sense): there will be occasions when the teacher may quite justifiably not be interested in exploring pupils' ideas and taking account of them in the development of the lesson. The teacher may feel the time is right to focus on scientific content, to introduce some new question or concept, or to redirect students' attention to the phenomena under investigation. The key is in the teacher's application of a varied repertoire of ways of using language as a tool for teaching and learning.

We can look at what this kind of discursive variety looks like in practice by using Sequence 4.5 below. It was recorded in a whole-class discussion session in an English primary school. The session followed a group-based session in which the children, in groups of three, had discussed a set of statements about the solar system and tried to decide if they were true or false. The sequence consists of two parts, taken from recordings at the beginning and end of the session respectively.

Sequence 4.5: Class 5 talk about the moon

Teacher: Keighley, would you read out number nine for us?
Keighley: (*reads*) 'The moon changes shape because it is in the shadow of the earth.'
Teacher: Right, now what does your group think about that?
Keighley: True.
Teacher: What, why do you think that?
Keighley: Hm, because it's when earth is dark then, hm, not quite sure but we think it was true.
Teacher: Right, people with hands up (*to Keighley*). Who would you want to contribute?
Keighley: Um, Sadie?
Sadie: I think it's false because when the sun moves round the earth, it shines on the moon which projects down to the earth.
Teacher: (*to Sadie*) Do you want to choose somebody else? That sounds good.

Sadie: Matthew.

Matthew: Well, we weren't actually sure cos we were (thinking) the actual moon (changes) which it never does or if it is in our point of view from earth which it put us in the shadow.

Teacher: That's a good point isn't it, it doesn't actually change, it looks as if it changes shape to us, that's a really good point.

(*We move now to later in the same session. The teacher has a large photo of the moon on the interactive whiteboard. She also has on a table a lamp (representing the sun) a globe (the earth) and a tennis ball (the moon.)*)

Teacher: Right look, if the sun's shining from here there is nothing between the sun and the moon, so from here on earth what we can see is a circle, a big shiny full moon. (*She holds the 'moon' so it is the third object in line with the 'sun' and 'earth'*) Right? That's a full moon, we can see the whole caboodle, if we're here on earth and the sun's over there. However, have a look now, what happens now. If I put the moon here (*she puts the 'moon' between the 'sun' and the 'earth'*) here's the sun, is there any light from the sun falling on this moon that we would be able to see from earth?

Children: No.

Teacher: What would we see if the moon is in that position?

Children: Nothing.

Teacher: Yeah, it would be totally dark. We get a completely black effect because we can't see it, we can only see it if there is light falling on it, and all the light is falling on this side and we're not over there, we're over here. Yes?

Child: If it's like that, the reason we can't see anything really because it's so dark around it.

Teacher: Yeah, it's dark, yeah, the light needs to land on it for us, it can't shine on itself. So that's when it's the darkest bit of the moon, we can't see it (*returns 'moon' to first position*). That's a full moon, over here relative to the earth, (*moves 'moon' to second position*) and that's when it's dark. However (*a child tries to interrupt*) wait a minute, let's get this right. If we come half way around (*she repositions the objects so that the 'moon' (ball) and the 'earth' (globe) are next to each other, facing the 'sun' (lamp)*) the sun's shining on this bit, but not on this bit, what would we see then?

Children: Half/half-moon.

Teacher: It would look like that. (*points at picture of half moon on whiteboard*)

Children: Yeah/ooh.

Teacher: Yeah, the sun's shining on that bit, but not on this bit we'd see a half moon. (*A child says 'ooh!'*) So that means that the moon is putting a shadow on itself, it's not the earth throwing a shadow on it, or a planet throwing a shadow on it, it's in its own shadow, if you like. The shadowy bit is just not lit up by the sun. And from earth we can only see about half of it, while the other half of it is this side. And this is how it works, (*she moves the 'moon' round the 'earth'. A child starts to speak but the teacher continues*) dark, half moon, full moon, half moon, and that's what happens. With those little crescents in between. (*Viola has her hand up*) Viola?

Viola: I've learned something now.

Teacher: Have you? Yeah (*laughs*) I'm a bit worried about what. Go on then.

Viola: I didn't know that, I know that you can't see the, the other half, but (*pause*) I don't know how to explain it (*laughs*).

Teacher: Maybe you need to give it a chance for it to sink in and think about it, it's quite hard to understand, I find it hard to understand.

In the first part of this sequence we see a teacher engaging with pupils in a way that has some 'dialogic' features, in the sense that this term is used by both Alexander and by Scott and Mortimer. In relation to Alexander's work we can see that students are given opportunities and encouragement to question, state points of view, and comment on ideas and issues that arise in lessons; the teacher's questions are designed to provoke thoughtful answers ('Why do you think that?'); the children's answers provoke further questions and form building blocks for further dialogue. Additionally, the students have the benefit of hearing each other's viewpoints and those who contribute undertake the useful exercise of having to try to express their ideas clearly. In Scott and Mortimer's terms, the talk is *interactive/dialogic* because the teacher engages the children in a series of questions, but these provide an opportunity for the children to express their own ideas. Moreover, the teacher does not make a critical assessment of these ideas as right or wrong, but rather takes account of them and allows the dialogue to continue. Through the use of interactive/dialogic dialogue, the teacher learns about the children's current understanding of the topic of the lesson and is able to use this information in developing the theme of the lesson.

In the second part of the sequence, the talk has a different pattern. Scanning over the sequence as a whole, it is quickly apparent that in the second part the teacher's talk takes up a much greater proportion of the dialogue. She uses these longer turns to explain to the children (with the use of the models of the earth, sun and moon) how the solar system generates the moon's phases. She again interacts with the children, but this time the questions are mainly used for different purposes – to check that the children are following her explanation, and to carry out some 'spot checks' on whether they have understood its implications, and so on. The dialogue here could be described as *interactive/authoritative*, though it is also *non-interactive/authoritative* in parts. In conjunction with the use of equipment, she uses language to provide children with information about the solar system that is absolutely necessary for their understanding of how it works. A multimodal presentation of this kind is an effective way of doing so – and it is likely that the students' fairly rapt attention to her demonstration was enhanced by their earlier opportunities to talk about the moon in their groups and in the previous interactive/dialogic episode. (We might note that at the end of the sequence one of the students comments, 'I've learned something now.')

In describing and evaluating the teaching in this lesson, it would be wrong to focus exclusively on either the early or the late parts of the dialogue. It is the quality of the dialogue as a whole that matters. A teacher can use different forms of 'communicative approach' at particular times, as appropriate. The crucial issue is whether the choices a teacher makes are effective for establishing and maintaining a collective IDZ, so that the dialogue supports the development of understanding for as many of the children in the class as possible.

We began by discussing the implicit norms or 'ground rules' that operate in classrooms. One well-accepted rule is that teachers can ask lots of questions; and another, in most classrooms, seems to be that students ask relatively few. Questioning is a natural and necessary part of classroom dialogue, and the relative extent to which teachers use questions does not distinguish very good teachers from those who are less effective. But a crucial difference between teachers seems to be how, when and why they use questions. While it is dangerous to generalize too widely, it does seem that this variation affects how well they help their students to learn. It seems that teachers whose students achieve the best learning outcomes regularly use dialogue to find out what children already know, to support and guide the children's activity, to monitor their engagement with the progress of a topic and to assess the development of their understanding. They also encourage more active and extended participation in dialogue on the part of the students. They use dialogue to effectively establish and maintain a collective IDZ for the duration of an activity, or even a whole lesson. In Alexander's terms, their teaching is 'dialogic'. This does not mean that they only generate the kind of classroom talk that Mortimer and Scott call 'interactive/dialogic'. Rather, it depends on teachers making good judgements about what kind of interaction is best suited for the occasion. Any of the types of dialogue in Mortimer and Scott's quadrant may be the most effective to use on any specific occasion.

The extent to which children themselves contribute to classroom dialogues is of course crucial – and it cannot necessarily be expected that they will recognize, or take up, opportunities for making more extended contributions when these are offered by a teacher. A valuable insight provided by Alexander's comparative research is into how the cultural contexts of schooling can shape both teachers' and students' expectations of the ways talk should be used as a tool for teaching and learning. The implicit ground rules that represent the ways participants expect classroom talk to happen can vary between education systems, schools and even the classrooms of particular teachers. It seems that teachers are rarely very aware of the ground rules that operate in their classrooms, and it is also rare for them to make a critical examination of the ways they use their prime teaching tool, spoken language.

To engage in dialogic/interactive talk with a teacher, students must know that the local ground rules of classroom interaction offer them legitimate opportunities to express their uncertainties and reveal their confusions, and to request information and explanations from the teacher. The value of children's educational experience may be affected by the extent to which their dialogue with the teacher enables them to appreciate the purpose of the activities they do, and how these activities fit together into a meaningful sequence of events. Research supports the view that a good teacher is not simply the instructor or facilitator of the learning of a large and disparate set of individuals, but rather the students' intellectual guide. This requires the establishment of the kind of learning environment that has been called a 'community of enquiry' (Lipman, 1970; Wells, 1999), in which they can take active and reflective roles in the development of their own understanding. This environment will be based on appropriate 'ground rules' for dialogue and will be maintained by teachers using certain kinds of dialogic strategies. In such classrooms, the students are apprentices in thinking, under the expert guidance of their teacher. For dialogic communities of enquiry to exist in many more classrooms, as we would suggest they should, there will need to be increased awareness on the part of teachers and teacher educators about the ways talk is used, and how it could be used.

Summary

There is no doubt that teachers can make a powerful contribution to the development of children as collective thinkers, and hence also to children's development as individual thinkers. By the ways in which they talk, act and structure classroom activities, teachers convey powerful messages regarding how learning and talking can be carried out. As the educational researcher Gee (2000, pp.201–202) puts it, 'Any efficacious pedagogy must be a judicious mix of *immersion* in a community of practice and *overt focusing* and scaffolding from "masters" or "more advanced peers" who focus learners on the most fruitful sorts of patterns in their experience'.

For children to become more able in using language as a tool for both solitary and collective thinking, they need involvement in thoughtful and reasoned dialogue, in which their teachers 'model' useful language strategies and in which they can practise using language to reason, to reflect, to enquire, and to explain their thinking to others. By using questions to draw out children's reasons for their views or actions, teachers cannot only help them reflect on their reasoning but also help them see how and why to seek reasons from others. By seeking and comparing different points of view, a teacher cannot only help those views to be shared, but also help children see how to use language to compare, debate and perhaps reconcile different perspectives. Providing only brief, factual answers to teachers' questions will not give children suitable opportunities for practice; but being drawn into more extended explanations and discussions of problems or topics will. This is the valuable kind of educational experience that dialogic teaching can offer. We will return to a consideration of teacher–student dialogue in Chapter 7.

Chapter 5

Learning to think together – and alone

In this chapter and the following we describe an approach to teaching children how to use language to think together. As you will see, by encouraging children's awareness and use of talk as a thinking tool, teachers can help them to develop intellectual habits that will not only help them in their study of the curriculum but should also serve them well across a diverse range of situations. At the heart of the approach is the negotiation by each teacher and class of a set of 'ground rules' for talking and working together. These ground rules then become established as a set of principles for how the children will collaborate in groups. The ground rules effectively open up and maintain an *intersubjective space* in which alternative solutions to problems are generated and allowed to develop and compete as ideas, without threatening either group solidarity or individual identity. We have described this approach in several other, earlier publications (in particular Mercer, 2000; Mercer *et al.*, 1999; Wegerif, Mercer *et al.*, 1999; Dawes, 2005; Littleton *et al.*, 2005): but in recent times we have extended its application to a broader age range of children and it has been used in a wider range of cultural settings. The work of other independent researchers has also enabled us to develop its principles and improve its procedures. As we will see in Chapter 6, there is now a strong body of evidence for its effectiveness.

Group talk in the classroom: how things normally are

In Chapter 3 we reviewed a range of studies that suggested that interaction between peers can be of potential benefit for children's learning, reasoning and problem-solving. However, we noted that classroom research has highlighted the seeming paradox of children working *in* groups but rarely *as* groups. Whilst they may be seated in close proximity, children frequently work alongside each other rather than with each other – their joint work, such as it is, being characterized by disagreements, disputes and turn-taking. That is, they may interact, but rarely 'interthink'. Moreover, it is not uncommon to see children seated in groups but working individually

(Bennett and Dunne, 1992; Galton and Williamson, 1992; Alexander, 2004; Dawes and Sams, 2004a).

It was the Spoken Language and New Technology (SLANT) project in the early 1990s that emphasised for us the disjunction between 'what is' and 'what could be' in relation to children's talking and working together in classroom settings. As described in more detail in Wegerif and Scrimshaw (1997), the SLANT researchers observed primary school children's (8- to 11-year-olds) talk when they worked together in small groups at the computer in classroom settings. Overall, 50 hours of classroom talk were recorded in ten Key Stage 2 primary school classrooms across five counties in the south-east of England. Detailed analysis of the children's joint sessions of work suggested that most of the interactions recorded were not task-focused, productive or equitable. In some pairs or groups one child so completely dominated the discussion that the other group members either withdrew from the activity, becoming increasingly quiet and subdued, or else they participated marginally, for example as the passive scribe of a dominant child's ideas. In other groups the children seemed to ignore each other, taking turns at the computer, each pursuing their own particular ideas when 'their turn' came round. Some groups' talk involved them in unproductive, often highly competitive, disagreements. From time to time these disagreements escalated, with the children becoming increasingly irritated with each other and engaging in vehement personal criticism. On the other hand, much group talk was relatively brief, somewhat cursory and bland. Particularly when groups of friends worked together, the discussions were uncritical, involving only superficial consideration and acceptance of each other's ideas. These observations resonated with those of other research projects, indicating that although grouping children was a common organizational strategy, talk of any educational value was rarely to be heard (for example Galton et al., 1980; Barnes and Todd, 1995; Bennett and Cass, 1988; Kutnick and Rogers, 1994). That said, very occasionally there was evidence of a distinctive kind of interaction that was qualitatively different and more educationally productive. Here the children engaged in discussions in which they shared relevant ideas and helped each other to understand problems. They were mutually supportive and were constructively critical of each others' ideas, with challenges and counter-challenges being justified and alternative ideas and hypotheses being offered. There was more of the kind of interaction that Barnes and Todd (1995) called 'exploratory'.

Building on Barnes and Todd's work in the analyses of the SLANT data (Fisher, 1993; Mercer, 1995), the researchers devised a three-part typology of talk, designed to reflect the different ways in which children in the project classrooms talked together:

- '*Disputational talk*', which is characterized by disagreement and individualized decision making. There are few attempts to pool resources, to offer constructive criticism or make suggestions. Disputational talk also has some characteristic discourse features – short exchanges consisting of assertions and challenges or counter-assertions ('Yes, it is.' 'No it's not!').

- '*Cumulative talk*', in which speakers build positively but uncritically on what the others have said. Partners use talk to construct 'common knowledge' by accumulation. Cumulative discourse is characterized by repetitions, confirmations and elaborations.

- '*Exploratory talk*', in which partners engage critically but constructively with each other's ideas. Statements and suggestions are offered for joint consideration. These may be challenged and counter-challenged, but challenges are justified and alternative hypotheses are offered. Partners all actively participate, and opinions are sought and considered before decisions are jointly made. Compared with the other two types, in exploratory talk knowledge is made more publicly accountable and reasoning is more visible in the talk.

The reader might like to test the application of the typology by considering each of the following short examples of discussions, Sequences 5.1–5.3 below (to which we will also provide a commentary). In all three of the transcripts below the participants are primary school children who are working at the computer. They are all engaged in the joint task of making up a conversation between two cartoon characters portrayed on a computer screen, and also have to decide what the characters are thinking as they speak. They then type the words into the relevant 'speech' and 'thought' bubbles. (Whenever it seemed to the researchers that the children were speaking the voices of the characters, the words have been placed in inverted commas.)

Sequence 5.1: Jo and Carol

Carol:	Just write in the next letter. 'Did you have a nice English lesson.'
Jo:	You've got to get it on there. Yes that's you. Let's just have a look at that. 'Hi, Alan did you have a nice English lesson. Yes thank you, Yeah. Yes thank you it was fine.'
Carol:	You've got to let me get some in sometimes.
Jo:	You're typing.
Carol:	Well you can do some, go on.
Jo:	'Yes thank you.'
Carol:	[*unintelligible*.]
Jo:	You're typing. 'Yes thank you' 'I did, yeah, yes, thank you I did.'
Carol:	You can spell that.
Jo:	Why don't *you* do it?
Carol:	No, because *you* should.

Sequence 5.2: Sally and Emma

Sally: Yeah. What if she says erm erm 'All right, yeah.' No, just put 'Yeah all right.' No, no.

Emma: No. 'Well I suppose I could.'

Sally: 'spare 15p.' Yeah?

Emma: Yeah.

Sally: 'I suppose.'

Emma: 'I suppose I could spare 50p.'

Sally: '50?'

Emma: Yeah. 'Spare 50 pence.'

Sally: '50 pence.'

Emma: '50 pence.' And Angela says 'That isn't enough, I want to buy something else.'

Sally: Yeah, no no. 'I want a drink as well you know I want some coke as well'.

Emma: 'That isn't enough for bubble gum and some coke.'

Sally: Yeah, yeah.

Sequence 5.3: Tina, George and Sophie

George: We've got to decide.

Tina: We've got to decide together.

George: Shall we right, right, just go round like [take

Tina: [No, go round. You say what you think, and she says

George: I think she should be saying 'Did you steal my money from me?'

Tina: Your go.

Sophie: I think we should put 'I thought that my money's gone missing and I thought it was you'.

George: 'I think it was you'.

Sophie: Which one?

Tina: Now what was it I was going to say, um, um.

George: No because she's *thinking,* so we need to do a thought. So we could write her saying.

Sophie: 'My money's gone [missing so'

Tina: [I was going to say if we're doing the one where she's saying, this is *saying* not thinking.

Sophie: 'My money's gone do you know where it is?'

Tina: No, [on the saying one she could say

George: [You should be saying.

Tina: Like she could be thinking to say to Robert, she could be saying, 'Do you know where's my money?' 'Do you know anything about my money going missing?'

George: Yeah, what, yeah that's good. When she's thinking I think she should be thinking, 'Oh my money's gone missing and its definitely Robert.'

Tina: Yeah.

Sophie: No cos she's *saying* it to him isn't she?

Tina: [No she's *thinking* at the moment.

George: [No she's *thinking*.

Tina: *That's* the speech bubble.

The talk in Sequence 5.1 has characteristics of disputational talk. Both participants take an active part, but there is little evidence of joint, collaborative engagement with the task. Much of the interaction consists of commands and assertions. The episode ends with a direct question and answer, but even this exchange has an unproductive, disputational quality. Sequence 5.2 has obvious features of cumulative talk. There is no dispute, and both participants contribute ideas that are accepted. We can see repetitions, confirmation and elaborations. The interaction is cooperative, but there is no critical consideration of ideas. Sequence 5.3 has some characteristics of exploratory talk. It begins with Tina and George making explicit reference to their task as requiring joint decision making, and they attempt to organize the interaction so that everyone's ideas are heard. They then pursue a discussion of what is appropriate content for the character's 'thought' and 'speech' bubbles in which differing opinions are offered and visibly supported by some reasoning (for example, 'No, because she's *thinking*, so we need to do a thought', '. . . if we're doing the one where she's saying, this is *saying* not thinking'). However, their reasoning is focused only on this procedural issue: they do not discuss explicitly or critically the proposed content of the character's thoughts and words. Were the space available to include longer examples, we could show that their later discussion also has some 'cumulative' features.

It is important to emphasize that the three-part typology described and exemplified above is not only meant to be descriptive: it has an evaluative dimension, reflecting our concern with educational effectiveness. Our analysis of children's talk supports the view that not all kinds of talk are of similar educational value. Talk of a mainly 'disputational' type, for example, is very rarely associated with processes of joint reasoning and knowledge construction. Whilst there may be a lot of interaction between children, the reasoning involved is mainly individualized and tacit. Furthermore, the kind of communicative relationship developed through disputation is defensive and overtly competitive, with information and ideas being flaunted or withheld rather than shared. It is common for this type of talk to comprise tit-for-tat 'yes it is', 'no it isn't' patterns of assertion and counter-assertion. Judgemental comments such as 'you're stupid' and 'don't do that, thicko' are typically heard. Disputational argument of this kind has little in common with the kind of reasoned argument that is represented by exploratory talk. Children engaged in a disputational type of talk are not orientated to the pursuit of reasoned argument, they are being 'argumentative' in the negative sense of squabbling and bickering.

In contrast to disputational talk, cumulative talk characterizes dialogue in which ideas and information are shared and joint decisions are made: but there is little in the way of challenge or the constructive conflict of ideas in the process of constructing knowledge. Cumulative talk represents talk that seems to operate more on implicit concerns with solidarity and trust, hence the recourse to a constant repetition and confirmation of partners' ideas and proposals.

Exploratory talk represents a joint, coordinated form of co-reasoning in language, with speakers sharing knowledge, challenging ideas, evaluating evidence and considering options in a reasoned and equitable way. The children present their ideas as clearly and as explicitly as necessary for them to become shared and jointly analysed and evaluated. Possible explanations are compared and joint decisions reached. By incorporating both constructive conflict and the open sharing of ideas, exploratory talk constitutes the more visible pursuit of rational consensus through conversation. Exploratory talk foregrounds reasoning. Its ground rules require that the views of all participants are sought and considered, that proposals are explicitly stated and evaluated, and that explicit agreement precedes decisions and actions. It is aimed at the achievement of consensus. Exploratory talk, by incorporating both conflicting perspectives and the open sharing of ideas, represents the more visible pursuit of rational consensus through conversations. It is a speech situation in which everyone is free to express their views and in which the most reasonable views gain acceptance.

The purpose of this three-part analytic typology is quite circumscribed: to focus attention on the extent that talk partners use language to think together when pursuing joint problem-solving and other learning activities. It is not designed to deal with many other important ways that the forms of talk reflect a variety of purposes used, such as the maintenance of social identities, expression of power and solidarity, emotional ties amongst speakers and so on (as studied extensively by sociolinguists, social psychologists and other researchers). The three types of talk were not devised to be used as the basis for a coding scheme (of the kind used in systematic observation research). We have had no wish to reduce the data of conversation to a categorical tally, because such a move into abstracted data could not maintain the crucial involvement with the contextualized, dynamic nature of talk that is at the heart of our sociocultural discourse analysis. Rather,

the typology offers a useful frame of reference for making sense of the variety of talk in relation to our research questions. While recognizing its relative crudeness, we have found that the typology is a very useful heuristic device. In an initial consideration of the data, it helps an analyst perceive the extent to which participants in a joint activity are at any stage behaving collaboratively or competitively and whether they are engaging in critical reflection or in the mutual acceptance of ideas. It is also very useful for helping teachers and others involved in educational practice gain insights into the functional variety of children's talk. Our original intention was to refine the typology into a more subtle and extensive scheme for differentiating talk in terms of its variety and adequacy for carrying out different types of joint intellectual activity, but our view now is that this would not be a particularly worthwhile development. It is hard to see what value a much more complex differentiation would offer, and the elegant simplicity of a three-part list would be lost.

Other educational researchers, working quite independently, have come up with very similar characterizations of intellectually stimulating, collaborative and productive classroom talk. In the USA, Anderson and colleagues (Anderson *et al.*, 1998; Chinn and Anderson, 1998) have identified the kind of talk they call *Collaborative Reasoning* (CR). On the basis of data they obtained through their own interventional studies, they say:

> During CR discussions, children express their positions, suggest new ideas, and challenge each others' arguments. . . . Empirical studies show that the quality of children's reasoning is high during CR discussions . . . and they display higher levels of thinking than in conventional classroom discussions. . . . In the course of CR discussions, children actively collaborate on the construction of arguments in complex networks of reasons and supporting evidence.
>
> (Kim *et al.*, in press)

It should be noted, however, that the source of such talk in their studies was *teacher-led* discussion with groups of children.

There are also strong links between the concept of exploratory talk (as we have defined it) and what some educational researchers have called 'accountable talk' (Resnick, 1999; Michaels and O'Connor, 2002). Resnick describes it as follows:

> Talking with others about ideas and work is fundamental to learning. But not all talk sustains learning or creates intelligence. For classroom talk to promote learning, it must have certain characteristics that make it *accountable*. Accountable talk seriously responds to and further develops what others in the group have said. It puts forth and demands
>
> knowledge that is accurate and relevant to the issue under discussion. Accountable talk uses evidence in ways appropriate to the discipline

(for example, proofs in mathematics, data from investigations in science, textual details in literature, documentary sources in history). Finally, it follows established norms of good reasoning. Accountable talk sharpens students' thinking by reinforcing their ability to use knowledge appropriately. As such, it helps develop the skills and the habits of mind that constitute intelligence-in-practice. Teachers can intentionally create the norms and skills of accountable talk in their classrooms.

(Resnick, 1999, p.5)

Drawing on their own extended work, as well as that of several other cognitive scientists, philosophers and discourse analysts, Keefer *et al.* (2000) also tried to identify the characteristics of the most productive classroom discussion when the subject matter is literature. They define a set of types of informal dialogue, which we summarize as follows:

1 *critical discussion*, which has the main goal of achieving shared understanding through accommodating divergent viewpoints and reconciling differences of opinion;
2 *explanatory enquiry*, which starts from a position of lack of knowledge with the main goal of overcoming this lack and identifying correct knowledge, using cumulative discursive steps;
3 *eristic discussion*, in which initial conflict and antagonism amongst participants is acted out through rhetorical attacks and defences of participants' own positions, and which may achieve some 'provisional accommodation';
4 *consensus dialogue*, which is discussion amongst speakers whose opinions are in agreement.

Discussing these forms of dialogue, they comment:

The dialogues' different starting points have different rules regarding the admission and management of dialogue commitments. For example, the dialogue commitments that are admitted into an inquiry aimed at explanation must show some promise of moving participants toward the goal of accurate or correct knowledge, as the criterion for success in this dialogue is ultimately whether assertions lead participants toward convergence on a problem solution. This condition does not hold for a critical discussion, which, having understanding and the accommodation of divergent opinions as a goal, affords participants the right to present their own moral or personal value judgments with the provision that they are held accountable for developing them within the constraints of the text and contributions of other participants. To deny a participant that right would be to violate the discursive norms that define this context of dialogue.

(Keefer et al., 2000, p.56)

These four categories do not neatly map onto our own typology, but there are some obvious connections between 'eristic discussion' and disputational talk; 'consensus dialogue' and cumulative talk. It would seem that exploratory talk subsumes characteristics of both 'critical discussion' and 'explanatory enquiry', though given the emphasis we have placed on group members achieving some kind of agreed conclusion to their joint enquiry, it is perhaps closer to the latter. We can also see that in their reference to 'discursive norms' in the quotation above, Keefer et al. are essentially invoking what we have called 'ground rules'. In relation to the particular curriculum focus of their research, they argue that 'critical discussion is the most appropriate dialogue type for a discussion focused on literary content' (p.58) and so they go on to use that dialogue type as a model for an evaluation of the discussions of groups of children aged around nine years old in a school in the USA. To do so, they developed a coding scheme that represented the ways that discussions proceeded through the contributions of each of the participants in a group. Their evaluative analysis was based on the view that:

> a productive discussion . . . should include some progress in the participants' understanding of the original question or issue being debated (e.g., participants ought to show greater interest in the development of ideas and issues than they do in the presentation and defense of their own positions). Furthermore, we believe that participants in discussions having these qualities might be more prepared to change their views – in other words, to seriously listen to (and even construct) arguments that run counter to views that they might initially hold.
>
> (Keefer et al., 2000, p.60)

We can see more clearly here some strong similarities between this notion of a 'critical discussion' and exploratory talk. Their analysis also examined the extent to which the relevant literary content was directly invoked and discussed by the groups. They concluded that the most productive literary discussions were those that included a high proportion of interpretive literary content. Although, as one would expect, the real talk in the groups they observed did not neatly fit into any of their four categories, they were able to identify the prevalence of talk most resembling 'critical discussion' with groups that engaged most with an interpretation of the literary content of their joint reading. They conclude by commenting on 'the challenge of helping teachers to lead discussions that are appropriate to the content and goals of the dialogue, scaffolding children to reason within the constraints of the dialogue rules and to initiate shifts in context when the content or the course of argumentation might warrant it' (p.79). This is the challenge that we will now go on to address.

The importance of exploratory talk

The kind of discussion we call 'exploratory talk' represents a *distinctive social mode of thinking* – a way of using language which is not only the embodiment of critical thinking, but which is also essential for successful participation in 'educated' communities of discourse (such as those associated with the practice of law, science, technology, the arts, business administration and politics). Exploratory talk thereby typifies language that embodies certain principles, notably those of accountability, of clarity, of constructive criticism and receptiveness to well-argued proposals, all of which are valued highly in many societies, particularly our own. Of course, there is much more involved in participating in an educated discourse than using talk in an exploratory way: the accumulated knowledge, the specialized vocabulary and other linguistic conventions of any particular discourse community have to be learned, and account has to be taken of members' prior contact, relative status and power. Also, there is not just one way of conducting a productive discussion or argument. We nevertheless maintain that exploratory talk embodies qualities that are a crucial, basic part of many educated discourses. Children need to know how to use language in this way to get things done, quite apart from the potential impact engaging in exploratory talk might have on their individual cognitive development and learning.

Observational research supports the conclusion that whilst exploratory talk constitutes a powerful way for children to think and reason together, they seldom talk in this way in school. This may be because of a lack of clarity on the part of teachers, and a lack of understanding on the part of children. When a teacher asks students to 'discuss' a topic, the teacher is almost certainly expecting a certain quality of interaction to take place, but these expectations are seldom made clear and explicit to the children. They are left to somehow work out what is required and what constitutes a good, effective discussion, but they rarely succeed in doing so. It is not that children cannot use language effectively as a tool for co-reasoning and 'interthinking', but rather that many do not know how to, or at the least do not recognize that this is what is expected of them.

As demonstrated some years ago now (Edwards and Mercer, 1987) and mentioned in Chapter 4, the norms or ground rules for generating particular functional ways of using language in school – spoken or written – are rarely made explicit. It is often simply assumed that children will pick these sorts of things up as they go along. But while picking up the ground rules and conforming in a superficial way with the norms of classroom life may be relatively easy, this may mask children's lack of understanding about what they are expected to do in educational activities and why they should do so. What is expected in terms of behaviour may be accepted without really being understood. The distinction between structures for classroom management (for example, lining up in pairs or sitting rather than kneeling on chairs) and structures for supporting learning (for example, listening to a partner or asking a question) may not be apparent to children. Even when the aim of talk is made explicit – 'Talk together to decide'; 'Discuss this in your groups' – there may be no real understanding of how to talk together or for what purpose. Many children may not appreciate the significance and educational importance of their talk with one another. They frequently assume that the implicit ground rules of the classroom are such that teachers want 'right answers', rather than discussion.

In the 1980s researchers such as Wells (1986) commented that the normative environment for talk in most primary classrooms was not compatible with children's active and extended engagement in using language to construct knowledge. This characterization of the classroom environment for talk is also one that emerges from more recent work by Alexander (2004, p.10), which has indicated that classroom discourse is 'overwhelmingly monologic' in form, as the orchestrators of classroom discourse (teachers) typically only offer children opportunities for making brief responses to their questions:

> if we are not careful, classrooms may be places where teachers rather than children do most of the talking; where supposedly open questions are really closed; where instead of thinking through a problem children devote their energies to trying to spot the correct answer, where supposed equality of discussion is subverted by . . . the 'unequal communicative rights' of a kind of talk which remains stubbornly unlike the kind of talk that takes place anywhere else. Clearly if classroom talk is to make a meaningful contribution to children's learning and understanding it must move beyond the acting out of such cognitively restricting rituals.
>
> (Alexander, 2004, p.9)

The use of language as a tool for collective reasoning is not a common topic for classroom talk or in school curricula. It is not very surprising, then, that little extended reasoning through talk by children is observable in most classrooms. This would seem to suggest that if children are to be empowered as thinkers and take a more active role in using talk to construct knowledge and understanding in class, teachers need to foster a different environment for talk in their classrooms. We have therefore responded to this need by developing a teaching programme designed to enable teachers to do just this: helping them shape and facilitate the use of discourse for the purpose of building understanding, enabling and encouraging the construction of personal meaning as well as shaping and confirming collective understanding.

It is not to children's benefit, or to that of society in general, that children should be expected to discover or infer this kind of important cultural knowledge for themselves or to live their social lives without it. Guidance can and should be provided by schools. Children cannot be expected to bring to educational tasks a well-developed propensity for reasoned dialogue. Using talking for learning and reasoning may require intervention, instruction and support. Children can be explicitly inducted into ways of talking and working together – it need not be expected to come naturally. From a sociocultural perspective, this identifies a distinct role for schools, which are cultural institutions supposedly created for guiding intellectual development. Education should help children to gain a greater awareness and appreciation of the functional language repertoire of wider society and how it is used to create knowledge and carry out particular activities. It should give them access to ways of using language that their out-of-school experience may not have revealed, help them extend their repertoire of language genres and so enable them to use language more effectively as a means for learning, pursuing interests, developing shared understanding and getting things done. A prime aim of education should therefore be to help children learn *how* to talk together such that language becomes a tool for thinking, collectively and alone.

It is important to help children to learn how to interact in classroom contexts – not least because it is possible that how a learner engages and interacts with others may potentially have a more profound and enduring impact on their circumstances than the acquisition of a better understanding of (for example) concepts associated with mathematics or science. The cultural tool of language does not just mediate teaching and learning, it mediates the broader culture too (Daniels, 2001). Thus careful consideration needs to be given to how children are inducted into ways of talking and working together.

In the next part of this chapter we will describe how, working with teachers, we and our colleagues have put these ideas into practice. We recognize, however, that there are some difficult problems to be faced in transforming this proposal into widespread educational practice. Barnes's early advocacy of the educational importance of talk of an 'exploratory' kind (Barnes, 1976; Barnes and Todd, 1977) found official endorsement in British education, in the Bullock Report (DES, 1975), through the National Oracy Project (The Open University, 1991; Norman, 1992) and eventually in the orders for the National Curriculum (for example DFE, 1995). But teachers face a real dilemma in trying to combine free and open discussions with their professional responsibility to teach a set curriculum.

Learning to reason together: The *Thinking Together* approach

Over the last 15 years or so we and our colleagues Lyn Dawes and Rupert Wegerif, in close collaboration with other researchers and teachers in the UK and elsewhere, have developed an approach to teaching called *Thinking Together*. Based on the sociocultural perspective that we have explained in this and earlier chapters, it is designed to ensure that children have educationally effective ways of talking and thinking together in their repertoires. Building on the Vygotskian notion of language as the prime cultural and psychological tool, it is an attempt to put a sociocultural theory of education into practice. To do so, it places a special emphasis on the role of the teacher as a guide and model for language use, who fosters an inclusive climate for discussion while also enabling children to understand better how language can be used as a tool for thinking. It supports children in learning to talk as well as providing them with opportunities for talking to learn. Through the systematic integration of both teacher-led interaction and group-based discussion children are helped to understand that aims for group activity and the use of spoken language are as much to do with high quality educationally effective talk and joint reasoning as with curriculum learning. The processes by which children learn how to learn are directly addressed, rather than being ignored or left to chance.

The *Thinking Together* approach rejects the static, objectified conception of knowledge associated with teaching as the transmission of knowledge. It is in accord with Alexander's view that 'knowledge and understanding comes from testing evidence, analysing ideas and exploring values rather than unquestioningly accepting somebody else's certainties' (Alexander, 2004, p.26). It requires children to become more meta-cognitive, aware of how they go about their learning and thinking, through enabling their participation in learning conversations, in classrooms where opportunities for dialogue with peers are frequent and where ground rules for exploratory talk are exemplified in the talk of the teacher.

For all age groups, children follow a series of *Thinking Together* lessons written by teams led by our colleague Lyn Dawes, in which the whole class is directly taught ways of using language as a tool for reasoning, with the aims for collaborative activity being made explicit in the teacher's whole class introduction to each lesson. The children are provided with well-designed activities for work in groups, in which they can practice applying and developing such skills. The activities include topics directly relevant to the school curriculum. Some take the form of computer-based activities using specially designed software (as explained in Wegerif and Dawes, 2004). During whole class plenary sessions, the children are guided by the teacher to reflect on both the nature and quality of their talk. Each lesson is designed to ensure a careful balance of teacher-led and group-based activities.

The teacher-led whole-class activities have been specifically designed to raise children's awareness of how they talk together and how language can be used in joint activity for reasoning and problem-solving. Given the proper opportunity, many (if not most) children in any class will be able to offer some sensible ideas about how to ensure that discussions are productive. As part of discussions about that topic, classes create and agree on a shared set of ground rules for talking together, to use when working in groups.

Thinking Together depends on children understanding that high quality speaking and listening is of great value in class; discussion should be inclusive and respectful of opinions and ideas; all relevant information should be shared; reasons should be requested and given and the group should seek to reach agreement. The children's ownership of the rules helps the groups to implement them. Additionally, children also become aware of some of the advantages of group work. For example, they come to recognize that listening to a range of ideas and comparing them can help everyone to come to a more reasoned decision; by learning how to think aloud together they are learning how to think clearly when working together and alone; helping others to learn is a way of coming to understand ideas; groups can generate shared memories through talk, available for later recall; talk allows everyone to reflect on both what they have learned and how they learned it; and they can often do better working together than working alone. Opportunities to evaluate, and where necessary revise, the ground rules are provided regularly throughout the lessons.

Whilst the precise nature of the activities undertaken by a teacher with the children may vary, in recognition of, for example, differential curricular demands and the age of the learners, some key principles embody the *Thinking Together* approach. These provide a framework for the direct teaching of the speaking and listening skills children and young people need, in order to learn from and with each other. So before moving on, we want to say a little more about some of these principles and why we think they are important.

The importance of collectively constructing ground rules for exploratory talk

As mentioned earlier, in the *Thinking Together* lessons teachers talk explicitly with children about what counts as good, productive discussion and together the children and their teacher collectively construct and agree some clear ground rules for making this happen in their particular classroom context. It is not the case that a set of predefined ground rules are somehow imposed upon children and their teacher. Rather, an agreed set of ground rules emerges from joint discussion and collective consideration by the children and their teacher of what makes for productive talk in their classroom context. As a consequence, these ground rules may partly reflect the particular 'local' concerns of the children and their experiences of productive/unproductive group activities. The agreed ground rules are then summarized in ways that the children both understand and identify with and are reproduced in the form of a poster, which is put up on the classroom wall to provide a constant source of reference. The rules generated by two of our project classes were as follows:

Our ground rules for talk (Year 4)

We have agreed to:

- share ideas;
- give reasons;
- question ideas;
- consider;
- agree;
- involve everybody;
- everybody accepts responsibility.

Our talking rules (Year 5)

We share our ideas and listen to each other.
We talk one at a time.
We respect each other's opinions.
We give reasons to explain our ideas.
If we disagree we ask 'why'?
We try to agree in the end.

Once the ground rules have been established in class they are there as common knowledge, which can be appealed to or invoked by the teacher or the children at any time. For example, by drawing their attention back to past shared experience, the teacher can try to ensure that the children enter subsequent talk activities with the appropriate frames of reference. As part of this process she may elicit educationally relevant past experience or knowledge from individual students, elaborating or reformulating what the child has said for the rest of the class. Such strategies are common linguistic tools of a teacher's trade. However, in this context such strategies are particularly effective because they are mobilized to guide children expressly and explicitly into effective ways of using language to think together. In this respect the whole-class plenary sessions constitute important opportunities for shared reflection on the appropriateness and value of the collectively agreed ground rules. If necessary these can be iteratively revised or reformulated to better capture the ways in which the children and their teacher want to talk and work together. This process of shared reflection also provides a distinctive way of explicitly 'talking about talk', which helps learners reflect on what makes educational dialogues effective and how best to learn through talk and joint activity.

Consensus and controversy

The *Thinking Together* group-based activities are designed so as to provide children with opportunities to work together in mixed-gender, mixed-ability groups to develop their speaking and listening skills. The children do not work in friendship groups, as a key aim of the approach is to ensure that children develop skills and resources that enable them to work with a range of different people – not just their close friends. Such group activities offer children good opportunities to practise and evaluate ways of thinking together away from the teacher's authoritative presence. Throughout these activities, which can only be completed successfully through talk and collaboration, the children are asked to collectively discuss issues and to reach a consensus regarding the solution to each problem set.

Some people have queried the importance that we place on groups reaching agreement. Their key concern seems to be that an emphasis on reaching consensus encourages conformity and acceptance and does not fully recognize that there are frequently irreconcilable differences between people's points of view. Surely, they say, it can be acceptable to agree to disagree: and may not a forced consensus be antithetical to the development of understanding? It is of course the case that many disagreements cannot be resolved and/or that people may agree to 'go with the majority' without really being convinced. But the imperative to reach consensus in the context of *Thinking Together* is designed to motivate the children to engage, and keep engaging, with each other's ideas and suggestions in a considered and critical way. Ironically, rather than encouraging a healthy diversity of opinion, the option of not reaching agreement can offer an easy way out of continued debate. As Claxton notes:

> Although consensus may be an appropriate ultimate aim, the voicing and consideration of alternative ideas, experiences and opinions may be essential if genuine understanding is to be achieved by all participants, and this applies not only to the topic in question but also to the grounds on which people can validly disagree.
>
> (Claxton, 2002, p.7)

By stressing that it is important that members of a group try to agree, rather than simply accept the view of the majority, the children are encouraged to explore fully all differences of perspective and the reasons given. They are not expected simply to concede points of view, comply with the majority or vote to reach a decision. As our colleagues Dawes and Sams

(2004a, p.100) put it: 'helping learners to collaborate in order that all might benefit is not just a matter of ensuring that everyone is placidly amenable or that disagreement is quickly stifled or avoided'. *Thinking Together* encourages children to confront and discuss differences of opinion, interpretation and understanding. As some eminent classroom researchers have also argued, 'disagreement is as important as agreement in keeping participants engaged in knowledge building . . . without some disagreement there would be no need to communicate and therefore no dynamic for change' (Wells, 1999, p.111), and, 'true dialogue entails challenge and disagreement' (Alexander, 2004, p.18).

Participants in *Thinking Together* collaborate but do not do not 'play it safe'. They confront and actively explore challenges, express diverse opinions, may raise controversial issues and explore different possible solutions to problems. The children and their teachers are enjoined to create, in and through their ways of speaking and listening, a secure and supportive context in which they are enabled to take the intellectual risks inherent in opening up their reasoning to others. It is important that children engaged in classroom-based discussions do not feel anxious, insecure or somehow personally 'at risk'. Intellectual risk taking flourishes when children are able to give voice to their ideas, secure in the understanding that the criticism of ideas is distinct from personal criticism. As we discussed in Chapter 3, such joint intellectual endeavours may enable them to take each other beyond what they were each capable of individually. Once children are enabled to challenge each other's suggestions, opinions and preferences without denying each other's personal competence, classrooms can become places of security and clarity rather than potentially threatening places of risk and ambiguity in which children have to devise strategies to cope rather than engage, as Alexander (2004, p.9) also argues. In such a climate, errors and mistakes can become stepping stones to understanding as opposed to potential sources of ridicule or humiliation: and children can talk confidently, listen and expect people to listen to them. The *Thinking Together* approach guides the construction of knowledge and it aims to do so through the creation of a positive culture of collaboration and community of enquiry in the classroom. As others such as Johnson and Johnson (1997), Underwood and Underwood (1999) and Elbers and Streefland (2000) have also argued, in such a culture of collaboration, founded on mutual respect and trust, learners feel able to take the risks inherent in opening up their thinking to their peer group. The emphasis on the importance of enquiry stresses the value of the critical consideration of a range of ideas, of discussion and negotiation based on reasoning. The debate and discussion of ideas may at times involve dispute and disagreement, but this is undertaken in an environment in which personal criticism is clearly distinguished from the criticism of ideas.

The role of the teacher

Whilst a concern with promoting effective reasoning in talk sits at the heart of the *Thinking Together* approach, the programme is predicated on more than just the establishment of 'ground rules' and the provision of suitable activities for children to work together on. The programme is designed to help children understand the rationale for the activities they engage in and take a more active role in constructing knowledge.

In this respect it is important to conceive of a teacher not simply as an 'instructor' or the 'facilitator' of the learning of a large and disparate set of individuals, but rather as someone who can use dialogue to orchestrate and foster the development of a community of enquiry in a classroom in which individual students can take a shared, active and reflective role in building their own understanding. Seen in these terms, the students are apprentices in collective thinking, under the expert guidance of their teacher. The quality of their educational experience, and perhaps their commitment to their own education, will be affected by the extent to which what they are doing in class has a continuity, a comprehensible purpose and scope for their own active participation. The teacher has to use classroom activities to develop Intermental Development Zones (IDZs) with students, and among students, to fulfil these conditions. So the success of the talk lessons depends on teachers creating communities of enquiry in their classrooms and using classroom activities to create IDZs.

Teachers make a powerful contribution to the creation of contexts for learning in their classrooms and the ways in which they talk, act and structure classroom activities convey powerful messages regarding how learning and talking are to be done in such contexts. Thus *Thinking Together* also involves the teacher modelling and exemplifying exploratory ways of talking for the children in whole class sessions – for example, asking 'Why?' at appropriate times, giving examples of reasons for opinions and checking that a range of views is heard. Also, in plenary sessions at the end of the lessons the teacher reviews with the whole class what has been done and what they might have learned from it. The organized continuity of this IDZ experience helps children to consolidate learning, gain educational benefits from their activity and hopefully see that the ground rules for exploratory talk do get good results. By using and modelling exploratory ways of talking the teacher is the children's discourse guide, showing them how to use talk to address problems and solve them.

There are now programmes of *Thinking Together* lessons for children of three age-groups 5–7 (Dawes and Sams, 2004b), 8–11 (Dawes *et al.*, 2003) and 12–14 (Dawes *et al.*, 2005). For illustration, one lesson plan from the programme for 5- to 7-year-olds is included as Appendix A. The lessons for all age groups are structured in a similar way. First, there is a teacher-led whole-class session, in which purpose of activities and aims for the lesson are set out explicitly. Aims for both the relevant area of curriculum study and for using language as a tool for thinking will normally be discussed. Next follows a group work session, in which children are specifically asked to think together about the task they have been given. Finally, there is another whole-class plenary session, in which outcomes from group work are shared, any questions arising are raised, and the teacher encourages reflective dialogue on the outcomes of the task and the quality of the group discussions.

In the group work session, the children are generally left to work alone. But observing and listening to group interaction provides a valuable formative assessment opportunity for the teacher, both in terms of gauging the level of children's understanding of curriculum topics and for judging the quality of talk within each group. Teachers can intervene as they see appropriate, but should avoid 'taking over' or staying involved for too long.

All of the activities in the programme (which usually runs for about 10 lessons) have some curriculum connection, but this is sometimes represented by a focus on the talk itself (as part of the English curriculum). All are designed to develop children's awareness of using talk and to allow them to practise using the ground rules in the context of an intrinsically motivating group activity.

So far we have talked in the abstract about the *Thinking Together* programme. To give the reader a feel for a *Thinking Together* activity in action we have reproduced a sequence of talk (Sequence 5.4) between a teacher and a group of 10- to 11-year-olds who are working in class on one of the activities that is especially popular with both the younger age groups. The activity, which is designed to enable the children to practise reasoning together using ground rules, involves deciding which of a set of pet animals is best suited to each of a particular set of owners. As Sequence 5.4 begins, the teacher has just intervened after listening to one group in her class talk for a short time. She approaches the group and joins the discussion:

Sequence 5.4: 'Which Dog?'

Teacher: Who are you trying to find a dog for at the moment?
Robert: Mrs Jenkins.
Teacher: Mrs Jenkins. Right. What do you know about Mrs Jenkins, Jane, so far? (*Jane does not respond*) You read it out to everybody?
Michael: Yeah.
Teacher: Right. What do you know about Mrs Jenkins so far? Who can tell me something?
Heidi: She's got a small home and a tiny garden, so she can't have a big dog.
Teacher: No, that wouldn't be sensible, would it?

Michael: And she can't. And she can't walk very far.
Teacher: Ah right.
Michael: So it has to be a very lazy dog.
Teacher: (*laughs*) Oh right! Good boy.
Robert: Sits by the fire. Look! (*points to a dog card*)
Teacher: Have you got a lazy, small dog?
Jane: We were thinking about Fifi. (*points to Fifi's card*)
Heidi: But this one – to be patted.
Robert: I think this one – to be patted.
Teacher: Why do you think that one? What's your reasons?
Robert: Well to, it was like, laying down, so that the lady could reach it.
Teacher: (*Reading*) Running and snow. It dislikes running and snow. It dislikes running, so yes, it would be quite a quiet dog. It likes to be patted by an old lady. That's quite a good reason. Why did you want Fifi, Jane? What were your reasons?
Jane: (*Silent*)
Another child contributes inaudibly.
Teacher: (*looking at Jane*) Can you remember? What did you think about that one? Pick up Fifi and have a good look. Is there a reason that you chose that for Mrs Jenkins?
Jane: Cos Mrs Jenkins has got a small garden and she needs a little dog.
Teacher: And you think Fifi's a little dog?
Jane: Yes.
Teacher: Yes, she does look little, doesn't she?

(adapted from Dawes and Sams, 2004a, p.105)

As can be seen in this extract, the teacher supports the work of the group of children, by encouraging them to share information about Mrs Jenkins and thereby underscoring the ground rule that all information should be shared. After the important criteria for the selection of the dog have been revisited, Jane begins to offer a suggestion, that Fifi might be a good choice. Heidi and Robert suggest another dog and explain their reasons. The teacher acknowledges their suggestions, but crucially redirects the discussion to Jane at this point, and supports her in her explanation of why Fifi might also be an appropriate choice. In this way the teacher has modelled another essential ground rule, that all alternatives and the reasons for them are considered before moving towards a conclusion. She avoids direct questioning of whether the group has done this, but through her intervention she reminds them of this rule and models ways to implement it. Thus the children learn to consider a variety of options and develop a collaborative orientation to their work.

We have already mentioned that each *Thinking Together* lesson typically has three main sessions or stages: an introductory, teacher-led, whole-class session, then small group activity and finally a whole-class plenary review.

To be effective, the whole-class introduction needs to be used to establish a shared understanding of the importance of group collaboration, and to share prior joint experience. Timely intervention in group talk helps to ensure that all are included, that difficult moments are overcome and that the talk remains focused on the activity in hand. The closing whole-class plenary can allow opportunities for sharing of ideas and for reflection on the effectiveness of the group. Groups can also share positive examples to illustrate how their talk contributed to their thinking (as explained in more detail in Dawes and Sams, 2004a).

One of the secondary (Year 8) teachers in our project schools was particularly good at guiding students' talk activities and modelling exploratory talk. She regularly revisited the ground rules and exemplified exploratory talk in whole-class sessions. One of her observed lessons, for instance, involved the use of a script for modelling exploratory talk. After introducing the script and reminding students of the nature of exploratory talk, she asked them to identify words that were features of exploratory talk, such as 'I disagree because . . .', 'Yes, although . . .' 'However . . .'. Students then had to decide in their talk groups whether a fictional character, Giorgio, would migrate from southern Italy to Milan. They had access to a set of cards that outlined various 'push' and 'pull' factors that would impact on Giorgio's decision making. Sequence 5.5 is an extract from the plenary that ended this lesson.

Sequence 5.5: A teacher guides and models the use of exploratory talk

Teacher: OK, who thinks that Giorgio will leave his home and migrate to Milan . . . Geoffrey?

Geoffrey: We all agreed that he would go because he supports Milan and he loves football.

Teacher: Does anybody agree with Gordon? Leanne?

Leanne: Yeah, we thought the same.

Teacher: Why? Gordon thought it was because of the Milan football team. Have you got another reason?

Peter: [in Leanne's group] We agreed with that but we thought it would be more important about the job . . . you know, the fact that he is likely to get a better job in Milan. That's more important than the football. And his girlfriend could get a job in Milan too because of the fashion industry there.

Teacher: Good. Now, do any groups disagree with Leanne and Gordon's group? Sam – see if you can use some of the language we discussed in the starter [*i.e. the lesson introductory session*].

Sam: We didn't, erm . . . OK. Although we could see that he would be really tempted by the job prospects we thought that the pull of his family and his friends, who all live in Potenza, would be too much. And his brother has already left home so Giorgio will feel even more guilty about leaving.

Leanne: But his brother sends money home – it says here [*reading*] 'People earn twice as much on average in Milan than in Potenza' so if Giorgio left, he could do the same.

This plenary continued for some time, with students using the information provided about 'push' and 'pull' factors as well as the talk words identified in the introductory session, to challenge and counter-challenge each other's views. The teacher can be seen modelling aspects of exploratory talk in her questions to the students. While reminding the students of the ground rules for exploratory talk, she asks the students for reasons for their decisions. She also asks them to consider each other's answers and if they disagree. The students, in turn, provide arguments for their decisions and constructively disagree with each other, giving their discussion some of the characteristics of exploratory talk.

It is thus important to ensure a balance between teacher-led, whole class sessions and talk groups in which children talk and work together without constant teacher supervision, on problem-solving activities. The organized continuity of this experience helps children to consolidate learning, gain educational benefit from their experience and hopefully enables them to understand how language can be used to get things done. The teacher is thus an orchestrator of discourse who continually works to foster a community of enquiry that both enables and encourages learners.

Computers as tools for developing interthinking

We mentioned in Chapter 3 that since they were first introduced into classrooms, computers have been mainly thought of as a means for individual children to access sources of information or to practise skills, rather than as tools for helping students work together. They have sometimes even been represented as offering children routes to 'personalized learning', which could liberate them from the teacher-guided, collective endeavours of the conventional classroom (Papert, 1980; Gee, 2003, 2004). In recent years, though, the communicative potential of computers has started to be appreciated, as shown by the shift (in the UK education community at least) from the acronym IT to ICT (Information and Communications Technology – with an emphasis on the C for 'communication'), and as explored by researchers such as Charles Crook (1994). In our view this has been a good move, not only because we have serious doubts about the real educational value of a highly individualistic, discovery/enquiry-led approach to education, but also because it uses the surprisingly strong appeal that computer-based work seems to have for children to encourage them to communicate while learning.

Since the earliest stages of the *Thinking Together* research in the early 1990s, we and our colleagues have been using computer-based activities within our intervention programmes for improving children's interthinking as they work together in school. This aspect of our research has been discussed in some detail by our colleagues Rupert Wegerif and Lyn Dawes in their book *Thinking and Learning with ICT* (Wegerif and Dawes, 2004). Some activities have used software specially designed (by Rupert Wegerif) for the purpose, while others have incorporated commercial software. Computer-based activities have been an important part of the methods we have used to encourage interthinking in English, citizenship, science and mathematics.

We will all have noticed that computers are sometimes treated by people as though they were sentient beings. For example, we say the computer 'asked me' for some information in order to proceed, 'won't let me' perform some action or 'can't find' a file. We get angry with them and describe them as 'stupid' or 'clever'. However, we all really know that they are just machines. Even young children show that they know that computers do not have the feelings and expectations of human conversational partners (Turkle, 1996). But it is because of their ambivalent nature – as being both an object (a machine or tool, that does what we make it do) and yet subject-like (a thinking being that processes information and can go wrong and make mistakes) – that computers can, with appropriate guidance and software design, play a unique and distinctive educational role.

Unlike real people, computers have the capacity to appear infinitely patient. Except in the specially designed environment of some computer games (which can encourage a 'beat-the-clock' mentality, antithetical to the reasoned process of problem-solving through discussion and enquiry) they do not 'mind' how long you take to respond. This potentially infinite patience of the computer is of special relevance when users are working not individually, but in pairs or groups (as in our own research). A pair of children who are 'asked' by a computer to provide a solution to a problem can take time to discuss their possible response together before keying it in. That is, they can introduce some discussion (D) between the computer's initiation (I) and their response (R). If the computer then provides them with evaluative feedback (F) on that response, we have a distinctive kind of pedagogic exchange – the IDRF (as Rupert Wegerif has described it: Wegerif *et al.*, 2003; Wegerif and Dawes, 2004) within which the users/ learners take on a more active and controlling role in the construction of their own knowledge. IDRF exchanges make good educational use of the computer's ambivalent nature. Through its initiations the computer can stimulate and direct the talk of the children towards curriculum-relevant problems, topics, concepts or procedures. In the discussion phase children construct their own meanings, to their own schedule. The computer then provides formative feedback on their joint efforts. Sequence 5.6 provides an example of such an IDRF exchange, taken from a dialogue recorded in a *Thinking Together* class.

Sequence 5.6: IDRF

The computer screen shows:
Q3
Rough surfaces cause
a) As much friction as a smooth surface?
b) More friction than a smooth surface?
c) Less friction than a smooth surface?

Rachel: Which one do you think it is?
Cindy: 'c.'
Rachel: I think 'b' (*laughs*).
Cindy: I don't. Look 'changes more surfaces than a smooth surface'. (*misreading the screen*)
Rachel: Yeah I know, but if you rub.
Cindy: (*inaudible*)
Rachel: Yeah I know but – wait, wait – listen, if you rub two smooth surfaces together right, will it be slippery or stable? (*rubs hands together*)
Cindy: Stable – depends how tight you've got it.
Rachel: Cindy listen! If you've got oil on your hands and you rub them together will they be slippery or not? (*rubs hands together*)
Cindy: Well you see (*She rubs her hands in a parody of Rachel but in a way that makes them miss each other*) cos they don't rub together they go.
Rachel: Cindy! (*in mock exasperated tone*) If you've got.
Cindy: Yeah, they will be slippery! (*laughs*)
Rachel: Yeah, exactly. So if you've got two rough surfaces and you rub them together it will not be as slippery will it?
Cindy: No.
Rachel: So that proves my point doesn't it?
Cindy: mmm.
Rachel: Yes, do you agree? Good. (*She clicks on answer 'b'*)
(*On-screen indication that 'b' was selected*)

(Adapted from Wegerif *et al.*, 2003)

Here two girls, Cindy and Rachel, are working together on a computer-based science tutorial. Rachel appears to know the answer to the question posed and eventually persuades Cindy that they should select option 'b'. She does so by giving reasons and drawing on the analogy of the effect of adding oil to one's hands when rubbing them. Note that it is only once

Cindy has agreed with the selection of option 'b' that Rachel uses the mouse to enter their answer. This extract indicates that whilst the computer interface is very simple and 'tutorial' in design, it has the potential to support a productive teaching and learning interaction through the IDRF structure of the talk. Instead of responding immediately to the computer prompt, the children take time to discuss and consider their possible response together and only when they have both agreed is their answer entered. In this case the *Thinking Together* context has transformed a potentially simple computer-user interaction into a complex, interactive learning experience.

As well as helping children prepare for collaborating at the computer, it is also important to give due consideration to the design of the software on which any activity is based. This is because the specific features and facets of software can affect the structure and pace of activity, thereby fundamentally transforming the cognitive and communicative requirements of learners' actions. However, software design is only part of a bigger picture. There is a tendency, not least amongst those in the computer industries, to assume that educational activities are contained in software. This is not the case. Software is just a resource, along with the hardware, the curriculum framework, the background knowledge of the participants and other situational factors, from which a computer-based educational activity can be generated in a classroom. Imagine comparing the different ways a programme for practising conversational Spanish might be used by (a) a class of children who had experience of speaking the language, had recently been on a visit to Spain and had often used similar software and (b) a class who had only ever studied formal Spanish grammar, had no conversational experience and had never used computers in their language study. (This kind of issue, but related to mathematics education, is discussed in practical terms in Sams *et al.*, 2000.) The same piece of software, used by different teachers and classes, can generate significantly different educational activities. So rather than conceptualizing computer-based activities as being in the software, we suggest a more realistic model would be as shown in Figure 5.1 (where the numbers of learners shown can of course be increased as appropriate).

The implications of this conceptualization of collaborative computer-based activity are several. For example, children who are skilled at collaborating may gain a very different experience from 'the same' computer-based activity than those who are not. The extent to which the computer-based activity is embedded in a continuing strand of work, rather than being an isolated, one-off event, can affect what knowledge students bring to a task, and what they gain from it. The strategies the teacher employs to engage children in the process of learning can be crucial. Recognizing this, our own work has stressed the importance of preparing children for collaborative activity at the computer by engaging teachers and children through

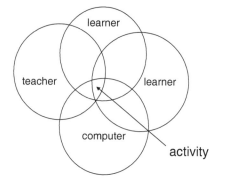

Figure 5.1 Conceptualizing computer-based activities

their participation in off-computer *Thinking Together* lessons. By discovering the usefulness of the ground rules in off-computer activities, they are prepared for using the same approach when they begin collaboration at the computer. This can transform what happens when children are asked to 'discuss' or 'talk together'. When computer activities are put into this context, they have much more potential for enabling collaborative learning.

Summary

The *Thinking Together* approach is about much more than delivering a particular form of communication skills training. It does encourage children to engage in particular ways of talking and working together, and they are explicitly guided in how to use language as a tool for reasoning together. They are encouraged to give reasons, seek clarification, ask questions, listen to each others' ideas and so on. But they learn much more than a model set of talk strategies, and the goal is not that they will simply adhere to the ground rules. The main goal is children's active appropriation of a particular educated way of talking and thinking, one that they understand and appreciate, so that in time they are able to apply, adapt and develop their use of language flexibly and creatively in their discussions. As we will explain in the next chapter, this also helps to develop their capacity for thinking alone.

Chapter 6

Evaluating sociocultural theory in practice

In this chapter, we will report the results of classroom-based research that has tested the effectiveness of the *Thinking Together* approach to classroom dialogue. It represents a major programme of work, over more than a decade, by the team listed in the Preface to this book. On a practical educational level, we have investigated the effects of establishing explicit ground rules for talk on children's language use, collaborative activity, reasoning and learning. We have also evaluated the teaching strategies and programmes of activities, designed for use with children of different ages and related to particular curriculum subjects. But no less important than these practical aspects has been the opportunity this research has provided to evaluate sociocultural theory as an account of the nature of learning and cognitive development. Vygotsky's ideas about the role of social interaction in cognitive development and the special significance of the tool of language, as we described in Chapter 2, have had a powerful impact on developmental psychology and educational studies. Yet this impact has been achieved despite the lack of much evidence in the form of observed, measured effects of social interaction on children's learning and development. Our research has now provided such evidence, specifically related to Vygotsky's proposal that collective thinking ('intermental' activity) shapes the development of individual thinking ('intramental' activity).

The research carried out in the UK by members of our research team has consisted of four main studies, involving children of three specific age groups: 6–7, 9–10 and 13–14. These age groups correspond to Year 2, Year 5 and Year 8 in the English school system, so we will use those headings to present the results. The first age group involved, and that which has been involved the most over the years, is Year 5, so we will begin with the research related to them.

Study 1: Effects on children's talk and non-verbal reasoning in Year 5

Our first substantial study was based in schools in Milton Keynes, in the south-east of England. We compared two sets of 9- to 10-year-old children: those in 'target' classes (in which teachers used the *Thinking Together* approach and children worked through the extended series of lessons, as described in Chapter 5) and those in control 'classes' (in similar schools that did not use *Thinking Together*, but who followed exactly the same pre-scribed National Curriculum course of study). One hundred and twenty-four children were involved. One of the key comparisons made was of the quality of children's talk, based on a detailed analysis of video-recordings of groups of target and control children participating in group-based activities.

Children in both target and control classes were also given a psychological test – *Raven's Progressive Matrices* (Raven *et al.*, 1995), which is commonly used as a general measure of non-verbal reasoning. It was designed to measure a person's ability to reason by analogy, independent of their language abilities and formal schooling. It is an excellent predictor of educational attainment and of occupational status. The test (of which there is more than one version) consists of a series of incomplete sets of geometric shapes. Children have to complete these sets of shapes in a logical manner. Its function in our research was to measure any effects that collaborative social activity might have on the development of children's ability to reason. We used the Raven's test to assess both the effects on children's *collective* problem-solving skills and also on their *individual* reasoning.

To deal first with collective reasoning: we gave children in both target and control schools, in groups of three, one version of the Raven's problems. We did this twice. The first time was just before the target children began the *Thinking Together* programme, and then again after they had completed the programme of lessons. We then compared the talk of children in the target and control classes, and the 'before' and 'after' talk of children in both sets of classes, as they carried out the Raven's test. These results suggested that *Thinking Together* was changing the ways that children used language as a tool for collective reasoning. There were striking differences between the two sets of children. Children who had participated in *Thinking Together* discussed issues in greater depth and for longer periods of time, participated more fully and equitably, more often sought justifications and provided reasons to support their views. (These findings are reported in detail in Mercer *et al.*, 1999 and Wegerif, Mercer *et al.*, 1999.) In a nutshell, we could see that the target children came to use more exploratory talk and their increased use of this kind of talk was associated with improved joint problem-solving.

To assess effects on children's individual reasoning, we gave a version of the Raven's Progressive Matrices test to each child in both the target and control classes (as an individual problem-solving activity), before and after the intervention programme in the target schools. The test results showed that the target children became significantly better at doing the problems *individually* when compared with the control children. That is, the children who had participated in *Thinking Together* appeared to have improved their individual non-verbal reasoning capabilities by taking part in group-based, and language-based, problem-solving activities. This is despite the fact that (a) the test is non-verbal: as mentioned earlier, it was expressly designed to be independent of language (and formal schooling); (b) the target children had no more experience or training in doing the Raven's matrices, together or alone, than the children in the control classes. We will provide some statistical information about the effects of *Thinking Together* on children's non-verbal reasoning when we describe Study 2. These results thus provided support for Vygotsky's hypothesis about the link between social activity and individual psychological development.

We gained some insights into the reasons for the improvements in the target children's group performances on the Raven's test by looking carefully at how their use of language changed as they tackled the test problems. A group of children in each target class had been video-recorded before and after the programme as they undertook the test. In this way we were able to observe, analyse and assess the target children's joint problem-solving activity at two stages – before they began to work according to the ground rules and after they had been doing so for some months. When we compared groups in target classes who had failed on specific problems in the pre-*Thinking Together* test with their successes in the post-*Thinking Together* test, we could see from the video-recordings and associated transcripts of their discussions how the quality of their collective reasoning was implicated. To illustrate this, here are two extracts of transcribed talk. They are of a group of children working on one of the Raven's matrices (D9). Sequence 6.1 was recorded before their participation in *Thinking Together* and Sequence 6.2 was recorded afterwards.

Sequence 6.1: Graham, Suzie and Tess doing Raven's Test Item D9 (prior to their participation in Thinking Together)

Tess:	It's that.
Graham:	It's that, two.
Tess:	Two is there.
Graham:	It's two.
Tess:	Two is there Graham.
Graham:	It's two.

Tess: Two is there.
Graham: What number do you want then?
Tess: It's that because there ain't two of them.
Graham: It's number two, look one, two.
Tess: I can count, we all agree on it? (*Suzie rings number two – an incorrect choice – on the answer sheet.*)
Suzie: No.
Graham: Oh, after she's circled it!

Sequence 6.2: Graham, Suzie and Tess doing Raven's test item D9 (after completing the programme of Thinking Together *lessons)*

Suzie: D9 now, that's a bit complicated, it's got to be.
Graham: A line like that, a line like that and it ain't got a line with that.
Tess: It's got to be that one.
Graham: It's going to be that don't you think? Because look all the rest have got a line like that and like that, I think it's going to be that because . . .
Tess: I think it's number six.
Suzie: No I think it's number one.
Graham: Wait no, we've got number six, wait stop, do you agree that it's number one? Because look that one there is blank, that one there has got them, that one there has to be number one, because that is the one like that. Yes. Do you agree? (*Tess nods in agreement*)
Suzie: D9 number one. (*She writes '1', which is the correct answer*)

In Sequence 6.1 Tess offers a good reason to substantiate her point of view but Graham ignores it and, perhaps upon being confronted with his stubbornness, Tess appears to 'give up'. Suzie has assumed the role of scribe and she says nothing until the end of the interaction when, having ringed the answer Graham wanted, she disagrees with it. Number 2 is not the correct answer, but the children nevertheless move on to tackle the next problem.

In contrast, Sequence 6.2 illustrates some of the important ways that these same children's talk changed after their participation in *Thinking Together* and how this helped them to solve the problem together. The discussion is noticeably more equitable, with all three children participating in the consideration of alternatives and the decision-making process. The children make more effective rhetorical use of language for expressing their opinions and persuading others of their value. Graham responds to opposition from Tess – giving a lengthy explanation of why he thinks 'number 1' is the right answer. This clear articulation of reasons leads the group to agree on the correct choice. Such explanations involve a series of linked clauses, resulting in longer utterances. In a number of ways, then, when compared with their earlier attempt, language is being used more effectively by the group as a tool for thinking together about the task they are jointly engaged in.

In this study, we used an innovative quantitative method for analysing changes in language use. We used a kind of software called a 'concordancer', as commonly used by language researchers, to count the relative incidence of key words and phrases in the transcribed talk of the children as they worked in groups. These key terms were those that our qualitative analysis had shown were associated with the use of exploratory talk. In this way we were able to compare the use of such terms by the same groups of children over the period of the intervention, and also to compare groups who had or had not been involved in the *Thinking Together* programme. Examples of such key terms are 'if', 'because', 'I think' and 'agree'. We searched for these in the combined transcript data of recordings for six groups of three children. Three of these groups were in target classes and three were in matched control classes, and each of these groups had been recorded before and after the intervention period as they tackled the Raven's problems. The results of this analysis are shown in Tables 6.1 and 6.2 below. An analysis of variance revealed that the difference between the target and control conditions was statistically significant (F = 5.547: one-tailed p = 0.039). In accord with the outcomes of the qualitative analysis, this supported the view that the intervention had changed the ways the children talked, and had done so in the direction intended by the intervention.

We will discuss the possible explanations for the target children's improved individual scores on the Raven's test, and the implications of these findings for understanding the relationship between language, social interaction and cognitive development, in more detail in relation to Study 2.

Table 6.1 Relative incidence of indicator words in the talk of focal groups in target and control classes while engaged in the Raven's test, before and after the implementation of the *Thinking Together* programme.

Indicator word	Target groups		Control groups	
	Pre	Post	Pre	Post
because/cos	62	175	92	66
agree	7	89	13	21
I think	51	146	31	52
Total	110	411	136	139

Table 6.2 Relative incidence of indicator words in the talk of focal groups in target and control classes during the Raven's test, before and after the implementation of the *Thinking Together* programme.

Indicator word	Target 1		Target 2		Target 3		Control 1		Control 2		Control 3	
	Pre	Post	Pre	Post	Pre	Post	Pre	Post	Pre	Post	Pre	Post
because/cos	25	100	12	45	25	30	34	25	28	17	30	24
agree	7	87	0	0	0	2	12	20	1	0	0	0
I think	7	87	0	12	44	47	27	44	3	5	1	3
Total	39	174	12	57	69	77	73	89	32	22	31	27

Study 2: Effects on talk, reasoning and studying science and mathematics in Year 5

The next study represents the largest evaluation to date of *Thinking Together*, and was also carried out with children aged 9–10. It focused on the potential benefits of improving the quality of children's talk and group-based learning for the study of science and mathematics. We also took this opportunity to replicate our investigations into the effects on children's talk and reasoning. This study is described in detail in several publications by members of the research team, including Mercer *et al.* (2004), Dawes (2004) and Mercer and Sams (2006). The project drew on research evidence that working in pairs or groups offers children good opportunities for developing reasoned arguments about mathematical problems (see, for example, Cobb *et al.*, 2000). In science education, such collaboration can be focused on practical investigations, which also have great potential value for helping children to relate their developing understanding of abstract ideas to the physical world. Computer-based science activities can offer similar opportunities in virtual environments. The research of Howe and Tolmie (1999), mentioned in Chapter 3, has shown that under certain conditions computer-based activities for groups of children are effective in promoting the development of scientific understanding: but this will depend on their discussions being productive and useful. To this end, our original intervention programme was redesigned for the present study. Once again, a key feature of the programme was the systematic integration of teacher-led interaction and group-based interaction. Several of the group-based activities made use of the science and maths education software that was commonly used by schools, some of which was provided to all English primary schools by the government.

The research involved, in total, 406 children and 14 teachers in schools in Milton Keynes. As in Study 1, the effects of the intervention programme on children's talk, reasoning and learning were studied through observation and formal assessment in experimental target classes, with pre- and post-intervention comparisons being made with children in matched control classes in other local schools with similar catchments. No special criteria were used to select teachers in target or control schools, other than their enthusiastic willingness to participate in research on children's talk. Seven teachers and their target classes of children in Year 5 (aged 9–10) participated actively by following the *Thinking Together* intervention programme.

The study involved the collection of our most comprehensive and varied data, as follows:

1   video recordings of groups of children in target schools engaged in joint activities during the implementation of the new version of the *Thinking Together* programme;
2   pre- and post-intervention video recordings of one group in each target and control class carrying out prescribed group-based activities;
3   video recordings of teacher-led whole-class sessions in target schools, during *Thinking Together* lessons;
4   for children in both target and control schools, their pre- and post-intervention scores on the Raven's Progressive Matrices test of non-verbal reasoning;
5   for children in both target and control schools, their pre- and post-intervention scores on tests of knowledge and understanding in science and maths (based on a set of assessment tasks for Year 5, known as 'optional SATs', which are made available to schools in England and Wales by the Qualifications and Curriculum Authority);
6   audio-recordings of interviews with teachers and children.

Effects on children's talk

As in Study 1, our investigation of changes in children's use of talk while engaged in group activities involved comparing the pre- and post-intervention talk of children in target classes, to see if they used more talk of an 'exploratory' kind and applied it productively to science and maths activities. We determined this through qualitative comparisons of the children's recorded talk. In order to ensure that this analysis was rigorous and valid, we also arranged for a blind assessment to be carried out. Two researchers not involved in the project, but who were familiar with the analytic method and with classroom interaction, also studied a substantial sample of this data, modified to eliminate all clues as to location and time of recording. They were asked to jointly (a) identify episodes of talk that had the characteristics of exploratory talk; (b) note the extent of these within the recorded event; and (c) use their findings to decide which discussions were pre-intervention and which were post-intervention.

The two sequences of talk below illustrate the kinds of differences observed between the talk of target and control groups. In the first example, a group in a control school are working on a computer-based science investigation into the effectiveness of materials for providing soundproofing.

Sequence 6.3: Control school group: Keep it Quiet

Hannah: (*reads from screen*) 'Keep it Quiet. Which material is the best insulation? Click "measure" to take a sound reading. Does the pitch make a difference?'
Darryl: No we don't want clothes. See what one it is then. (*points to screen*)
Hannah: No it's cloth.
Darryl: Oh it's cloth.
Hannah: Go down. This is better when Stephanie's in our group.
Darryl: Metal?
Hannah: Right try it.
Deborah: Try what? That?
Hannah: Try 'glass'.
Darryl: Yeah.
Deborah: No one.
Hannah: Now.
Darryl: (*interrupts*) Measure.
Hannah: Now measure. Hold. (*Turns volume control dial below screen*)
Darryl: Results, notes.
Hannah: Results. We need to go on a different one now. Results.
Darryl: Yeah, you need to go there so you can write everything down.
Hannah: I'm not writing.

For comparison, the next transcript is of a group of children in a target school, who have been involved for two terms in the *Thinking Together* programme. They are engaged in a very similar computer-based activity to that of the control school group, but in this case about the effectiveness of materials for blocking out light.

Sequence 6.4: Target school group: Blocking out light

Ross: OK. (*reads from screen*) 'Talk together about a plan to test all the different types of paper.'
Alana: Dijek, how much did you think it would be for tissue paper?
Dijek: At least ten because tissue paper is thin. Tissue paper can wear out and you can see through, other people in the way, and light can shine in it.

Alana:	OK. Thanks. (*to Ross*) Why do you think it?
Ross:	Because I tested it before!
Alana:	No, Ross, what did you think? How much did you think? Tissue paper. How much tissue paper did you think it would be to block out the light?
Ross:	At first I thought it would be five, but second –
Alana:	Why did you think that?
Ross:	Because when it was in the overhead projector you could see a little bit of it, but not all of it, so I thought it would be like, five to block out the light.
Alana:	That's a good reason. I thought, I thought it would be between five and seven because, I thought it would be between five and seven because normally when you're at home if you lay it on top, with one sheet you can see through but if you lay on about five or six pieces on top you can't see through. So that's why I was thinking about five or six.

The talk of the group in Sequence 6.3 indicates that the children are not working collaboratively except at the most superficial level. They do not share knowledge, build on each other's suggestions, provide reasons for their proposals or seek joint agreement. The contributions are monosyllabic and minimal. It does not seem that the participants are at all engaged with one another's thinking. This kind of talk is not uncommon in primary class-rooms and illustrates a need for the guided development of children's skills in communicating and thinking together. In Sequence 6.4, on the other hand, the children's discussion has many of the features of exploratory talk. They ask each other for information and opinions, seek reasons and provide them, share their thoughts, and evaluate proposals that are made. Challenges are constructive and all the members of the group are involved in working towards a joint decision. The children's use of the structures they have recently been taught may seem a little formulaic (for example, Alana's repeated 'Why do you think that?'); but they are using the strategies appropriately and purposefully. Opinions are treated with respect. Each speaker has the opportunity to develop their ideas as they speak. Indeed, it appears that the talk constitutes thinking.

These two transcribed sequences are illustrative of the kinds of differences that we observed between the talk of children in control schools and those in target schools, and between the pre-intervention and post-intervention talk of the same groups of children in target schools. The reliability of our pro-cedure for identifying these differences was confirmed by the two researchers who carried out the blind assessment exercise, as they correctly identified the transcribed discussions as pre- and post-intervention for five out of the six classes.

Table 6.3 Year 5, relative incidence of indicator words in the talk of groups in target classes during the same activity, before and after the implementation of the *Thinking Together* programme.

Indicator word	Pre-intervention	Post-intervention
because/cos	13	50
I think	35	120
would	18	39
could	1	6
Total	67	215

In this study we again compared the relative incidence of key words in the children's talk, before and after the intervention, while carrying out the same activity. The results are shown in Table 6.3.

It can be seen that there is a greatly increased incidence of the words indicative of exploratory talk in the children's discussions after the intervention. The children's greater use of such words reflects their increased attempts to reason collectively before deciding on a course of action and moving on through the activity. Our qualitative observations had also shown that the more children explain and justify their views, the longer their utterances will tend to be. We therefore counted the number of utterances in the talk data for target groups that exceeded 100 characters (a figure chosen on the basis of our first, informal consideration of the data) when transcribed. This excluded text read by children from the computer screen. The results of this analysis, provided in Table 6.4, are indicative of the more elaborated contributions to the discussions made by children post-intervention.

Table 6.4 Year 5, relative incidence of long utterances in the talk of groups in target classes during the same activiy, before and after the implementation of the *Thinking Together* programme.

	Pre-intervention	Post-intervention
Utterances of more than 100 characters	1	46

Effects on children's reasoning

To assess changes in children's reasoning, we again used Raven's Progressive Matrices. The mean scores of children carrying out the Raven's test are

Table 6.5 Year 5, group performances of children on the Raven's test, before and after the implementation of the Thinking Together programme.

	Pre-intervention: mean scores	Post-intervention: mean scores
Target classes	20.08	23.62
Standard deviation	4.05	2.41
Control classes	19.90	22.36
Standard deviation	3.42	2.29
Effect size	0.55	

$F_{(1, 76)} = 6.281$; two-tailed $p = 0.014$

shown in Table 6.5. It can be seen that the target pupils performed significantly better than the control pupils after the intervention, taking into account the pre-intervention performance levels of both groups.[1]

The results for the groups are strongly indicative of the intended effect of the intervention. The mean scores are shown in Table 6.6. The target children performed significantly better than the control children after the intervention, taking into account pre-intervention performance levels.[2]

Our previous studies had shown statistically significant increases in individual scores on the Raven's tests. These new results provide evidence of changes in both group *and* individual reasoning. They therefore provide further and stronger support for the sociocultural hypothesis that using language as a tool for reasoning collectively can influence the development of individual thinking and learning. They also support our more specific hypothesis that a programme of activities for encouraging the use of exploratory talk can have specific, predicted positive effects on the quality of children's reasoning. It is worth noting that, as in Study 1, the target children were no more familiar with the test than the control children. This therefore supports the view that the talking and reasoning skills gained by the target

Table 6.6 Year 5, individual performances of children on the Raven's test, before and after the implementation of the Thinking Together programme.

	Pre-intervention: mean scores	Post-intervention: mean scores
Target classes	16.26	18.90
Standard deviation	3.98	3.54
Control classes	15.60	17.88
Standard deviation	4.36	3.70
Effect size	0.27	

$F_{(1, 224)} = 6.065$; two-tailed $p = 0.015$

children were not highly task-specific or context-bound, but represented a transferable competence. It seems that the children had gained generalizable skills of the kind that education should provide.

When we consider why the target children improved their reasoning as individuals, more than one kind of explanation seems possible. One explanation is that from their group activity over the period of the intervention, they became better at sharing knowledge. When they did the Raven's test as a group exercise after the intervention, they were able to use these improved communication skills to learn new, successful problem-solving strategies from their partners, while also learning from having to justify and make explicit their own strategies for doing the test problems. They then were able to apply these strategies in the individual test situation (because for all the groups, the group tests preceded the individual tests). But a more intriguing possibility is that the children had not only improved their communicative language skills and so learned better specific strategies for dealing with the Raven's problems: they might have improved their reasoning skills by 'internalizing' the ground rules of exploratory talk, so that they became able to carry on a kind of silent rational dialogue with themselves. That is, the *Thinking Together* activities and associated teacher guidance may have helped the target children to become more able to generate the kind of language-based rational thinking that depends on the explicit, dispassionate consideration of evidence and competing options. Such an interpretation is consistent with Vygotsky's claims about the link between the social and the individual; collective thinking has a shaping influence on individual cognition:

> The greatest change in children's capacity to use language as a problem solving tool takes place ... when socialised speech is *turned inward*; ... language takes on an intrapersonal function in addition to its interpersonal use.
>
> (Vygotsky, 1978, p. 27)

We will return to consider these different possible types of explanation as part of our overall conclusions in Chapter 8.

Effects on children's knowledge and understanding of the mathematics and science curricula

The results of the assessments of the two sets of children's study of mathematics are shown in Table 6.7. The results show that the children in the target classes improved their attainment in maths significantly more than those in the control classes. These results, together with more informal evidence from teacher assessments, support the conclusion that the intervention was effective in improving children's study of the maths curriculum. In their

Table 6.7 Year 5, students' scores on the mathematics curriculum assessment, before and after the implementation of the *Thinking Together* programme.

	Numbers of children	Pre-intervention: mean scores	Post-intervention: mean scores
Target classes	109	2.43	5.53
Standard deviation		1.86	2.45
Control classes	122	2.39	4.20
Standard deviation		2.00	2.23
Effect size	0.59		

F (1, 228) = 28.394; two-tailed p = 0.000

recorded comments to the research team, the teachers in target schools also reported that the children generally engaged more collaboratively, enthusiastically and productively in the group activities.

The results of the assessment based on the science curriculum are shown in Table 6.8. The numbers of children are less than the total number who participated, because to ensure validity of statistical analysis it was necessary to exclude those children for whom no pre/post match was possible due to departures during the project and absences at the times of testing. It was also unfortunate that, because of staffing problems in one school at the time of the post-intervention assessment, one class had to be excluded. Nevertheless, the results indicate that the scores of target classes increased significantly more than those of the control classes. This supports the view that the intervention had a positive effect on the target children's study of the relevant parts of the science curriculum.

Overall, the results show that the children in the target classes gained significantly better scores in science and mathematics than those in control classes, thus providing evidence for the effectiveness of the intervention in improving children's study of the curriculum. The results of Study 2 provide

Table 6.8 Year 5, students' scores on the science curriculum assessment, before and after the implementation of the *Thinking Together* programme.

	Numbers of children	Pre-intervention: mean scores	Post-intervention: mean scores
Target classes	119	3.97	5.70
Standard deviation		2.32	2.42
Control classes	129	4.22	5.04
Standard deviation		2.00	2.21
Effect size	0.29		

F (1, 245) = 10.305; two-tailed p = 0.002

strong evidence that teaching children how to use language as an effective tool for collaborative activity has a significant and beneficial effect on their educational participation and achievement.

Study 3: *Thinking Together* in Year 2

Following the success of *Thinking Together* with 8- to 12-year-olds, our attention then turned to consider the potential value of the approach with younger children, aged between 6 and 7 years. The series of *Thinking Together* lessons developed specifically for use with this younger age group have been published as *Talk Box* (Dawes and Sams, 2004b). The *Talk Box* lessons are based on the key *Thinking Together* principles described earlier in the chapter, but the learning and teaching are based on more concrete resources and the associated activities require minimal reading and writing so that the children can concentrate on using spoken language.

Over the course of a full academic year we worked with six teachers (and their learning support assistants and head-teachers in three target schools) who adopted the *Thinking Together* approach in their classrooms (for full details see Littleton *et al.*, 2005). These teachers used the *Talk Box* lessons as an initial basis for their work and subsequently devised their own additional activities for their Year 2 children. Throughout the year we made video-recordings of interactions between teachers and their classes. We also recorded children working together on the activities of the programme. After the intervention, teachers, language support assistants and head-teachers in participating schools were interviewed about their experiences.

The interviews with staff showed that they evaluated their involvement very positively, even in the one school in which the implementation had, due to staffing problems, been difficult. In particular, they showed an increased awareness of the nature and functions of talk amongst participating teachers, and of the importance of improving children's communication skills as a means for ensuring their successful participation in education. We found the positive responses of the head-teachers particularly valuable because, although they had agreed to *Thinking Together* being adopted within their school, they were less immediately involved with the approach on a day-to-day basis. On completing a lesson about Florence Nightingale, one head-teacher commented:

> Now, I've done that lesson with Year 2 last year and it was very difficult getting questions from them, questions that you'd get information from. I did it this year and it's incredible, the questioning – and I think it's really developed that skill of questioning. Because that's quite a difficult and mature skill to have, quite complex. In fact it was really interesting, because once we had watched the video and the

children had asked the questions, when we came to learn about Florence Nightingale, because they had asked the right questions they were able to get so much more information.

This was echoed by another head-teacher, who noted:

I was quite impressed with the way that they are working together . . . they are listening to each other, taking turns and asking. They are working things out together where before – I have not noticed that. In those particular sessions (*the lessons observed*) I have noticed that they have all been engaged in what they are doing.

She contrasted this with the previous state of affairs:

Based on previous knowledge of these classes at this school I wouldn't have expected children to have the skills to enrol other members of the group who weren't engaged initially, bringing in other children into what's happening not just ignoring them . . . I wouldn't have expected to see so many children listening to each other involving each other actually, even noticing that somebody else hasn't given any input, and I think that I certainly haven't witnessed that any where else before.

Issues of social inclusion also figured prominently for the teachers and head-teachers. One head-teacher made this observation of a group of children:

They didn't assume that what one child said was the answer. They were very keen to know what each individual child knew, and that was really good. In another group, within the same lesson, there was a child who has a statement, and again, the inclusion there was excellent. So I think it seems to work across, for all children, I suppose – special needs children, EAL (*English as an Additional Language*) children, the more able children. . . . There's one little girl who's both EAL and special needs and to see her animated in a lesson is just wonderful.

This seemed to indicate that for learners who might otherwise have found it difficult to contribute to group-based learning experiences, explicit discussion of ground rules for talking and working together has the potential to foster a positive, inclusive and supportive learning environment, based on mutual respect and trust. In order to pursue the issue of inclusion and participation we used the video data to make a detailed case study of an initially silent child, Nuresha, for whom English was an additional language.

A case study: Nuresha, Vijay and Kyle

Nuresha was a child in one of the target schools from a Bengali-speaking family. Vijay had a similar background, though he was more fluent in English. Kyle was a native English speaker of local origin. When we analysed our initial video-recordings of the group working together on Raven's Matrices, it was noticeable that Nuresha did not speak at all. On the recording she could be seen sitting well back from the table, while the other group members, Vijay and Kyle, worked on the task. Sometimes she looked round the room, sometimes she played with her ruler but she was completely disengaged from the group. The teacher introduced the group task and asked questions to check for understanding. She asked Nuresha several questions, such as: 'Do you agree, Nuresha? What do you think? Can you see why it's not number 3?' In response Nuresha nodded. When the teacher left the group Vijay took over the pencil and answer sheet. Kyle said it was his 'go' and a little later asked Nuresha if she wanted a go. Nuresha shook her head. Neither of the other children spoke directly to her again during the rest of the sequence. The subsequent exchange between Kyle and Vijay was disputational and involved disagreement over who should answer each question. There was no explanation of opinions or collaboration to work out the patterns in the puzzles. Sequence 6.5 below is illustrative of the children's talk before their participation in *Thinking Together*. The group are working on one of the Ravens' Progressive Matrices test items.

Sequence 6.5: It's four not five

Kyle: It's four not five (*referring to the numbers of two of the figures they could choose to complete the set*).
Vijay: We're on number five now, bogey. Look, we done number four, dumb brain. It's this one, isn't it?
Kyle: No.
Vijay: It's this one isn't it?
Kyle: No.
Vijay: Yes.
Kyle: No.
Vijay: It's number one.
Kyle: No. It's my turn to cross it off.
(*Kyle attempts to take the pencil from Vijay who keeps it and marks number one on the answer sheet. Kyle raises a fist to Vijay and Vijay runs away from the table saying 'Don't hit me'.*)

In this extract, the boys disagree without attempting to explain, provide reasons for opinions or seek each others' views: this is archetypal disputational talk. The competition between them is not productive from an educational point of view. Their main aim seems to be to assert or defend their individual ideas and there is no attempt to pursue the task collaboratively.

Shortly after this extract was recorded, the teacher began the programme of *Thinking Together* activities. The next recording we made of Nuresha was about half-way through the project in a whole class setting. In this session Nuresha was better engaged with the task and appeared much more comfortable in the group. She responded appropriately and confidently in response to a question from the teacher and took part in class activities such as miming happiness to a partner. Towards the end of the academic year we video-recorded Nuresha, Vijay and Kyle again, undertaking exactly the same Raven's Progressive Matrices problem as in Sequence 6.5. Sequence 6.6 is a sample of their group's talk.

Sequence 6.6: Which one?

Kyle:	Which one. . . . (*to Nuresha*) You have to ask us which one we think. OK. You have to say, 'Kyle and Vijay, whose name, which one?'
Vijay:	You have to say, 'I don't want to do this' or 'Kyle, what do you think?', say.
	(*And a little later*)
Vijay:	Next. Nuresha's getting the best ones, isn't she? You have to say 'What do you think, Vijay or Kyle ?'
Nuresha:	I think that. (*indicating figure two*)
Kyle:	I think that. (*indicating figure four*)
Vijay:	Nuresha, look.
Nuresha:	I think, that, that, that.
Kyle:	No, because, look, because that goes round (*points to figure*). It goes out. It goes out.
Vijay:	Or that one. (*points to figure*)
Kyle:	No, because it hasn't got squiggly lines.
Vijay:	It has to be that.
Kyle:	OK number four.
Nuresha:	Number four.

This time the way that they worked together was quite different. The video showed all members of the group leaning forward to the table and frequently looking at each other as they pursued the task, and Nuresha was involved throughout. The children decided as a group that each should take turns at handling the task materials and ticking the answer sheet. The children reminded one another of some of the ground rules for talking that had been agreed in their class. In this extract it can be seen that Nuresha is much more involved in the group's shared reasoning. She is encouraged by the other two children, who are listening to one another and accepting alternative viewpoints better. Nuresha suggests an alternative that challenges Kyle and Vijay, prompting Kyle to provide reasons why her suggestion may not be the correct answer to the puzzle. When the group converge on an answer, Nuresha affirms her participation by repeating the answer aloud, echoing Vijay. Nuresha speaks 26 times in this second recording. This is less than the others (Kyle 72 and Vijay 76) but is obviously significantly more than the pre-*Thinking Together* session. She is involved in all the decisions that are made. She is asked one question in the pre-intervention session, but 21 in the corresponding post-intervention session. 'What do you think?' is the commonest form of question, several times taking the form 'What do you think, Nuresha?' All three children display a readiness to work together and an understanding of the importance of each individual contribution to the group's answer. Their interaction resembles exploratory talk.

This case-study highlights the value of explicitly establishing ground rules for classroom talk, so that previously tacit understandings concerning appropriate ways of working and talking in classroom contexts become accessible and an exploratory way of talking becomes part of the repertoire of all children. Children like Nuresha, who for a variety of reasons may be almost silent in the classroom, can be helped to find a voice. The process may be self-conscious at first, and may involve the children deliberately using particular model phrases, strategies or techniques in a slightly formulaic way. But this represents a vital entry into the discursive work and life of the classroom – a crucial basis on which to build. Furthermore, children such as Kyle and Vijay can be helped to understand that they have a responsibility to ensure that all those with whom they work are able to contribute their ideas to joint discussions and debates. As Wells reminds us, in school-settings:

> The tasks and modes of discourse that tend to be privileged are precisely those that are least familiar to non-mainstream children; as a result, a situation is created in which these children become educationally disadvantaged.
>
> (Wells, 1999, p.40)

If we are to ensure that children's unfamiliarity with ways of talking and relating in the classroom does not become a basis for their educational disadvantage, talking for learning has to be given explicit attention.

In Study 3, we again used a concordance analysis to measure the frequency of key words that the qualitative analysis showed were associated with children's use of talk of an exploratory kind. The changes in language use and in the ways that children interacted, as illustrated by the case study

Table 6.9 Year 2, target classes: relative incidence of indicator words in the talk of groups in target classes during the Raven's test, before and after the implementation of the *Thinking Together* programme.

Indicator words	Pre-intervention talk	Post intervention talk
because/cos	9	36
I think	23	31
if	2	13
why	3	12
which	9	21
what	15	21
you (used in questions)	31	144

of Nuresha's group, were confirmed by this analysis. The results are summarized in Table 6.9.

It can be seen that use of key terms found to be important indicators of language being used to reason together and encourage the inclusion of other's perspectives increased over the period of the intervention in the target classes. We undertook the same analysis in relation to the talk of three groups recorded in three control classes in schools who had not participated in the programme. The children's talk in the post-intervention period showed no similar pattern of change. The results are summarized in Table 6.10. It can be seen that there was no similar increase in the use of those words.

Taken together, these findings indicate that children as young as 6 and 7 can improve their ability to use talk for reasoning, if they are given specific guidance by their teachers. Another way of outing this is to say that raising children's awareness of the ground rules of classroom talk and how they can be modified enables them to become active participants in the collective processes of knowledge construction. In this way, children at the start of their school careers can be helped to find a voice in the classroom, such that

Table 6.10 Year 2, control classes: relative incidence of indicator words in the talk of groups in control classes during the Raven's test, before and after the implementation of the *Thinking Together* programme.

Indicator words	Pre-intervention talk	Post-intervention talk
because/cos	15	21
I think	35	17
if	0	7
why	0	1
which	12	2
what	8	7
you	5	11

they can engage with and enjoy the process of negotiating meaning and constructing understanding.

Study 3: *Thinking Together* in Year 8

Our most recent work has been in secondary schools in the UK, involving a new *Thinking Together* programme specially designed for the age group 13–14 and the Year 8 curriculum, focusing particularly on the study of geography, history and English (in order to take account of recent national curriculum initiatives for humanities subjects; the programme of lessons is published in Dawes *et al.*, 2005). Again we examined changes in the talk and academic performance of students in two target schools (who engaged in *Thinking Together*) and students in another matched control school (who pursued their usual activity over the duration of one school year). We recorded children in the target schools before and after the intervention as they worked together in groups on specially designed activities, so as to observe any changes in their use of language for joint problem-solving. In terms of individual development, we focused on students' study of the English curriculum, using students' individually written responses to a problem selected from a bank of assessment material for English in Year 8 provided to schools as part of the National Curriculum. This problem was related directly to the curriculum that had been studied in both target and control schools. It required students to assess the persuasive quality of non-fiction texts (public service advertisements).

Once again, concordance software was used to compare the transcribed pre-intervention and post-intervention talk of groups in the target schools with that of groups in the control school, recorded at the same time. The relative rates of incidence of key terms – 'because', 'agree', 'if', 'I think' and 'so' – associated with exploratory talk were counted. This revealed that the incidence of key words in the target schools more than doubled in the post-intervention recordings. In contrast, over the same period of time, the incidence of these words in the talk of the groups in the control school diminished. The results of this analysis are summarized in Table 6.11. (Note: one group in School 2 was not available for the post-intervention recording and so is not included. Obvious repetitions by speakers were counted as one instance (i.e.: If, if you would that . . .) and we did not count instances of the key words where they could not be seen to be associated with reasoning.)

The results of the analysis of the changes in the talk of students are illustrated by Sequence 6.7. It is taken from the talk of a group in a target school before the start of the *Thinking Together* programme. The students were carrying out the Year 8 English assessment task mentioned earlier. They were given two public service newspaper articles about driving safely (entitled 'Slow Down' and 'Safe Speed') and were asked to decide together

Table 6.11 Year 8, relative incidence of indicator words in the talk of focal groups during the English assessment task, before and after the implementation of the *Thinking Together* programme.

School	Pre-intervention		Post-intervention	
Control	because/cos	9	because/cos	2
Nine students in three groups	agree	0	agree	0
	I think	3	I think	7
	if	5	if	0
	so	0	so	4
	Total	17	Total	13
Target 1	because/cos	8	because/cos	39
Nine students in three groups	agree	0	agree	2
	I think	6	I think	30
	if	0	if	17
	so	1	so	10
	Total	15	Total	98
Target 2	because/cos	2	because/cos	11
Seven students in two groups	agree	0	agree	4
	I think	3	I think	10
	if	2	if	4
	so	0	so	3
	Total	7	Total	32

which one would be the best for achieving the intended outcome of encouraging drivers to drive more slowly in urban areas.

Sequence 6.7: Talk of Year 8 students in a target school before the Thinking Together *programme*

Joseph: I think this one's (*inaudible*).
Sofia: Yeah. It says like to protect the children and this one doesn't say anything like that.
Joseph: Mm.
Julian: Um, well this one (*'Safe Speed'*) is an argument about it could be a huge accident with cars but this one's protect the children and houses (*inaudible*) so I reckon this one. (*all giggle*)
Sofia: Yeah.
Joseph: I think this one.
Sofia: Yeah.

We can see that in Sequence 6.7 the discussion is very short (less than ten seconds). The students immediately agree with one another, copying each other's arguments and there is no real consideration of alternative views.

There is no evidence of the group members using this opportunity to reason collectively. The next example is of the same group after participating in *Thinking Together*, again discussing the two texts.

Sequence 6.8: Talk of Year 8 students in a target school after the Thinking Together *programme*

Joseph:	I think the voice of the Daily News article (*'Slow Down'*) is more persuasive because it talks about um (*pause*)
Sofia:	Children.
Joseph:	Yeah, children getting run over, not people in general.
Julian:	Yeah, people are more receptive to like things like that I think.
Sofia:	Yeah – cos they've got more chance of getting hit cos they're not as aware as adults.
	(*And a little later*)
Joseph:	Not if they're accelerating at 30 mph then, if they're near a school, if like it's home time and they walk through the gate then phutt! They're dead.
Julian:	Yeah but like if, if there was a crash like on the road here (*illustrates with hand on table*) then all these cars would have to stop and if someone was, like, talking on the mobile or something they wouldn't have time and they'd crash and then someone, the [person
Sofia:	[Yeah.
Julian:	behind and there'd be a chain reaction.
Joseph:	Yeah but it would be more spaced out on the motorway.
Julian:	Not necessarily.
Sofia:	No, not with all the traffic jams.
Joseph:	They've got way more lanes.
Julian:	Yeah but not in rush hour, it's still full up.
Joseph:	Yeah but they.
Sofia:	Like in the morning when everyone's going to work and when they come back.
Joseph:	Yeah true. (*long pause*) I do think this one's (*'Safe Speed'*) good though because it actually has quotes from people like this Inspector Jones.
Julian:	Yeah rather than this one's (*'Slow Down'*) kind of question and answer. It's just like, it's like, well, not really (*pause*).
Joseph:	It's like telling you what to do. This one's more persuasive (*'Safe Speed'*) and this one's (*'Slow Down'*) telling you but I still think this one's (*'Safe Speed'*) more . . . (*points to paper*)

Julian: But erm, down by my old school there was about, like, five bumps coming up to the school, if they did that on all the schools, things could be a lot more safer.

Joseph: True. (*long pause*) So, I think in general, this (*'Slow Down'*) is more persuasive.

Julian: Yeah, the idea of the kids, of vulnerable kids, walking home from school, is much more persuasive.

Sofia: Mm (*nodding*)

Joseph: Yeah.

Julian: We're all agreed then.

There is a striking contrast between the two sequences. Compared with Sequence 6.7, in Sequence 6.8 the students engage in a much longer, deeper discussion of the newspaper texts and their discussion has many characteristics of exploratory talk. The students reason together about the task, giving arguments for their opinions, evaluating alternatives, and reaching agreement in the end. They are not afraid to disagree, but in doing so give reasons and justifications for their disagreement. Speakers listen to each other's arguments, as indicated by their responses.

The next example, Sequence 6.9, comes from a recording in the control school, made at the same time as Sequence 6.8 and the other post-intervention recordings in the target schools. These students did not participate in the *Thinking Together* programme and – although they have had the same amount of school experience as the children in the target schools – it can be seen that their talk is similar to the talk of students in the target schools *before* the programme.

Sequence 6.9: Talk of Year 8 students in a control school

Simone: I prefer that one. (*'Slow Down'*)

Adam: It tells you what (*pause*) people (*pause*) just say slow down.

Amanda: Anyway we have [to

Simone: [It's saying, erm, that you have to slow down near schools (*inaudible, laughing*)

Simone: Whereas

Adam: Yeah, that one. (*'Slow Down'*)

Amanda: That one.

(*The students then give up the task*)

Sequences 6.7 and 6.9 are a reminder of how educationally unproductive classroom discussion can be when students have had no guidance in how to talk and work together. As mentioned earlier, an assessment of effects on individual students' study of the curriculum was made from their performance on an English curriculum assessment task of a similar kind (but with

Table 6.12 Year 8, students' scores on the English assessment task, before and after the implementation of the *Thinking Together* programme.

School	Number of children	Mean pre-intervention score	Mean post-intervention score	Difference
Control	91	3.62	3.37	−0.25
Target 1	71	4.38	7.28	2.90*
Target 2	57	6.35	7.65	1.30*

* Indicates a statistically significant change $F (2, 215) = 61.0$; at $p = 0.05$. There was no significant difference between the target schools.

different content) to that which all students in Year 8 encounter, and which in the target schools they would have tackled in their group activities. The analysis showed that, over the same time period, students in target classes improved their scores significantly more than students in the control classes. These results are presented in Table 6.12.

The scores in the target schools showed a statistically significant improvement, while those in the control school did not. The results thus support the view that the *Thinking Together* programme enhanced students' achievement in English, and once again are suggestive that the guided experience of collective thinking can have a positive shaping influence on individual learning and development.

Thinking Together in different cultural contexts

As part of our evaluative research, we have worked with Mexican colleagues (Sylvia Rojas-Drummond, Manuel Fernández Cardenas and their colleagues at UNAM) to explore the utility of the *Thinking Together* approach in state primary schools in Mexico. The Mexican educational context differs from that of the UK in some relevant ways. Historically, there has been little interest in either groupwork or educational dialogue. This is reflected both in the curriculum and in the physical layout of the classrooms, which all have desks in straight rows facing the front. It was vital to ensure that the UK model was not used inappropriately as a prescription for how teaching and learning should be done in the cultural context of Mexican primary schools. Differences between Mexican and UK cultural habits of argumentation, particularly when it comes to expressing disagreements, also needed to be taken into account when establishing appropriate ground rules for talk. The adaptation of the *Thinking Together* programme for the Mexican context was therefore a challenge. Whilst the core programme of activities was derived from the original *Thinking Together* lessons, the programme also included extra materials, games, texts, objects for use in experiments, activity cards, answer sheets and software that are relevant to and appropriate for use with Mexican fifth and sixth graders (10–12 years).

The Mexican studies made similar use of the Raven's Progressive Matrices test as the UK studies. The results show that the *Thinking Together* intervention led to significantly improved scores for individuals in the target classes, akin to the results observed in the UK. Comparisons of the children's talk pre- and post-intervention also revealed that after participating in the *Thinking Together* programme the children used longer utterances (made up of chains of clauses in order to provide evidence and reasons) and made more frequent use of 'porque' (because) as they provided explicit reasons. (For more details see Fernández *et al.*, 2001/2002; Rojas-Drummond and Mercer, 2004.)

The findings from Mexico suggest that, with culturally sensitive and appropriate adaptation, the *Thinking Together* approach is of value and relevance to children and teachers who are working in markedly different educational contexts to those encountered in the UK. Helping children to talk together in educationally productive ways is of course, an international concern. At the time of writing, the programme is being used and evaluated with children aged 6–8 in Japan, by Futoshi Hiruma and his colleagues at Kansai University, and preliminary results are very encouraging. Other studies are beginning at the University of Utrecht, led by Ed Elbers and Mariette de Haan, focusing on the talk and reasoning of children from different ethnic and cultural backgrounds. In England, in a large project involving a community of schools in North Yorkshire called *Talk for Learning*, our Cambridge colleague Robin Alexander has been introducing key elements of the *Thinking Together* approach into a professional development scheme for encouraging dialogic teaching.

Some critical concerns

Having described the evidence in support of the *Thinking Together* approach, we should also deal with some criticisms or concerns about it that have been expressed by teachers and researchers. In Chapter 5 we explained that at the basis of the approach is the establishment of a set of ground rules for talking by a teacher with their class. During presentations and professional development workshops, we have sometimes heard worries expressed by teachers about our insistence on the establishment of these explicit rules for talk. Some teachers have been concerned that children already have so many sets of rules to contend with in school, that to impose yet more on them is undesirable. However, what is required is not really the imposition of a new, alien set of rules but rather – as everyone is implicitly operating some set of 'rules' about how to interact – an agreement on which ground rules should apply. As two of our colleagues have explained:

Problems arise for groups when participants have different ideas of what ground rules operate. Such talk may end with people feeling that others have been dominant, assertive and unreasonable, or that individuals have been too quiet, and have not contributed. These things happen in groups in many settings – not just classrooms. The *Thinking Together* approach rests on raising awareness of the importance of joint ground rules and then helping groups to work within rules decided by the whole class.

(Dawes and Sams, 2004a, p.98)

Children's own responses to bringing the norms for discussion out into the open are generally positive. Here are some comments by children (aged 10–11) from classes involved in the *Thinking Together* research:

It has helped us if we are working in groups – now we've got the rules for it as well it's made us think, 'Oh, if one person's talking we can't barge in and talk in front of them'. . . . We normally take it in our turns and say 'What do you think?' instead of leaving someone out. . . . (I'm not) afraid to challenge someone with their answer – (I) don't just sit there and say 'All right – *pick* that one. I don't care'. (It) makes us feel more confident if we're in a group.

Some children's comments refer to the value of exploratory talk for helping to assess various alternatives before reaching decisions:

Before the project, if we'd been sitting in the group and got one answer we'd say like – 'Oh just say it's that' but now we've been thinking, 'Oh let's think of another answer it could be as well', not just . . . saying 'Oh it looks like that one'. Try each.

Some reported that they learned more by pooling their ideas than by working alone:

It's easier to work in a group than it is on your own because then you've got the time to talk to the person you are working with. . . . If you both get the same answer you know it's got to be right because two people have got more chance than just you working it out on your own. . . . Even if you do get it wrong you've got it wrong as a group and not just as a person.

Some researchers have made a rather different kind of criticism, which is that children do not need guidance and instruction on how to use language as an intellectual tool, and indeed that there are good reasons why this should not be done. For example, Lambirth (2006) argues that the ground rules associated with exploratory talk have no intrinsic value as a basis for collaborative activity, they simply reflect the language habits of the more privileged, educated members of society. Proposing that children should use more exploratory talk is, he maintains, simply an assertion of the superiority of middle-class culture and a denigration of the language habits of working-class children's communities. Having to make a shift from existing sets of ground rules (those that may operate in the child's out-of-school experience) to those related to exploratory talk will, he suggests, undermine the linguistic identities and communicative self-confidence of many children. Moreover, he argues, learning new ways of using language will not provide most children with routes to greater success in society, because socio-economic factors will prevent their social mobility. So rather than empowering children in their communicative and cognitive activity and enhancing their development, it is concluded, the *Thinking Together* approach will instead reinforce social equalities and disempower children from less educated backgrounds.

It seems that in making such attacks, no critics have actually questioned the quality of our data or the validity of our analysis of it. There has been no refutation of our claims that the target children in our studies come to use more exploratory talk, solve problems more successfully together and improve their individual scores on tests of reasoning and curriculum attainment. Nobody has provided classroom data of their own to counter our claims about the generally poor quality of children's talk in groups in the absence of such interventions, or to support the claim that being encouraged to follow the ground rules will lower some children's self-esteem. And no account has been taken of children's own positive evaluations of participating in *Thinking Together* (as reported above). Moreover, it seems to us that underlying the kinds of criticisms made by Lambirth and others are some serious misunderstandings about language.

First, there seems to be an implicit assumption that encouraging children to take up a new set of norms (the ground rules) for their classroom discussions necessarily means telling them that they should give up other normative, habitual ways of talking (or at the very least devalue them). But this subtraction model of language learning, which proposes that adding any new language genre to a child's language repertoire must involve the deletion of some existing genre, has no scientific foundation.

Second, these criticisms seem to confuse two kinds of language variation: on the one hand there are the varieties and dialects of a language such as English, as used in different communities; and on the other there are the various genres of any language which are used in different kinds of situation. The first type of variation is represented by differences between American and British standard varieties of English, or by differences between the regional dialects and accents of northern and southern England. It essentially represents differences of form, not function. The other is represented by the differences between a formal, rational debate amongst scientists in a seminar and their chat about life afterwards in the bar; or by the differences between someone asking a stranger for directions and an intimate conversation between lovers. This is a functional type of variation. Confusion between these two kinds of variation was prevalent in debates about the educational relevance of the work of Basil Bernstein (1971) so many years ago. Language scholars have tried to address, and correct, this kind of confusion for years (see for example, Halliday, 1978; Wells, 1999; Cook, 2003), but it seems they will still have to go on doing so.

To relate this confusion to our own concerns: it is perfectly possible for exploratory talk to be enacted in Cumbrian dialect, Jamaican patois, Standard British English, or any language of the world. It can be spoken in an English accent that is middle class Australian, working class Glasgow, or from rural Alabama. The same applies to disputational talk. There is of course an association between the use of certain dialects and some genres, which reflects the association of particular varieties with particular social worlds (so that a scientific paper presented in Cumbrian dialect would be a rare and interesting novelty), but that does not mean the two kinds of variation cannot be distinguished. Indeed, for educational purposes it is absolutely vital that they are.

It would be good if schools taught children to understand the nature of this kind of sociolinguistic variation, and it is unfortunate that they often do not. Rather, schools have traditionally contributed to the denigration of non-standard dialects (and some regional accents). It is both unnecessary and unfortunate that some children are led to believe that their local English is inferior or inadequate. But this is a different matter entirely from encouraging the use of exploratory talk. Helping children to develop the skills of rational debate is simply extending their range of functional speech genres. It need have no detrimental effect on their affinity to the language variety of their home community, and indeed should have no bearing on their attitude towards it; though it should certainly help them feel more empowered and at ease in a wider range of social situations.

Regarding the possibility that most children's out-of-school experience will provide them with all the necessary language skills for getting things done in society, so that they need no special guidance on this in school, all available evidence suggests that this is not the case. As discussed in Chapter 5, our own data has shown that the natural occurrence of talk of an exploratory kind during group activities in the classroom is very rare. Naturalistic studies of children's informal talk in and out of the classroom also do not provide evidence of its occurrence. For example, in her ethnographic study of children's informal language, Maybin (2006) recorded the talk in school of 23 British children aged 10–12 over a period of some months, by asking some of them to wear radio-microphones as they went about their school lives (in and out of class, including play periods and conversations with the researcher). As she remarks, her data shows that children 'slip easily in and out of the speech genres in different contexts' (p.32). Her findings are a testament to the natural fluency, creativity and functionality of children's language – but her report of her research includes no examples of dialogue that resembles exploratory talk. There are no good reasons to believe that all, or even most, children will encounter much of the kind of rational discussion typified by exploratory talk in their out-of-school lives. If that is so, and we do not hear them making use of it when they are asked to work and talk together, we cannot assume that they have it in their repertoire.

We turn next to the critical argument that *Thinking Together* ground rules represent not the language base for the development of rational thinking, or even a useful language genre for solving problems, but merely an arbitrary set of middle-class language habits. This might carry some weight if we had not found that the use of the ground rules improved children's cooperative and individual success in solving the problems of the Raven's Progressive Matrices. The results of that test, designed to measure cognitive ability independent of children's linguistic and educational background, show that something was happening other than the adoption of some rules for polite bourgeois conversation. As a result of the intervention, children also improved their attainment in mathematics and science, seemingly through their improved use of language as a tool for learning. It is not clear how critics can dismiss these findings, except by saying that they do not consider improved reasoning skills and educational attainment worthwhile achievements.

Summary

Evaluations of *Thinking Together* indicate not only that the programme impacts positively on children's collective problem-solving, but that it also enhances their individual reasoning capabilities too. The research has thus provided unique evidence to support Vygotsky's claims about the relationship between language use, social interaction and intellectual development, as explained in Chapters 1 and 2. Our findings show that group activities can offer learners good opportunities to practise and evaluate ways of using language to think collectively away from the teacher's authoritative presence. Children seem to enjoy gaining more awareness of how language is used as a tool for reasoning and they appreciate the effects it has on their collective activity. But for these beneficial effects to occur, they need guidance of a specific kind. The *Thinking Together* intervention programme was carefully designed to include both group-based peer group activities and teacher guidance. The success of its implementation supports the view that the development of understanding is best assisted by a careful combination of peer group interaction and expert guidance. Our findings indicate that if teachers provide children with an explicit, practical introduction to the use of language for collective reasoning, then children learn better ways of thinking collectively and better ways of thinking alone.

More generally, our results enhance the validity of a sociocultural theory of education by providing empirical support for the Vygotskian claim that language-based social interaction (intermental activity) has a developmental influence on individual thinking (intramental activity). More precisely, we have shown how the quality of dialogue between teachers and learners, and amongst learners, is of crucial importance if it is to have a significant influence on learning and educational attainment. By showing that teachers' encouragement of children's use of certain ways of using language leads to better learning and understanding, we have also provided empirical support for the sociocultural conception of education as a language-based process for inducting children into new communicative and cognitive practices.

We are living in times when our culture is undergoing radical change and the demands of the future cannot be readily anticipated. It is therefore imperative that education, in offering an effective preparation for life, orients to the crucial challenge of helping children develop learning skills and dispositions that will enable them to thrive on uncertainty. By harnessing the power of talk for reasoning and learning, children become more able to engage sociably and effectively with others, to benefit from reasoned dialogue with their teacher and peers, and ultimately to be empowered as learners with the reasoning capabilities necessary to rise creatively to the challenges posed by an uncertain future. We have shown that there are practical ways of making this happen in school.

Notes

1 Pre- and post-intervention comparisons of groups of children in the target and control classes working on the Raven's test were made using an analysis of covariance with pre-intervention results as covariate, post-intervention results as dependent variable and condition as fixed.

2 Pre/post comparisons of individual children in the target and control classes doing the Raven's test were also made using an analysis of covariance with pre-intervention results as covariate, post-test results as dependent variable and condition as fixed.

Chapter 7

Time for learning

Classroom dialogue in its temporal context

If you can look into the seeds of time,
And say which grain will grow and which will not,
Speak then to me . . .

(*Macbeth*, Act I, Scene 3)

In the early chapters of this book, we described a sociocultural theoretical perspective on teaching, learning and development and explained why we thought it provided a useful basis for understanding the functions of dialogue in the classroom. In the later chapters, we have shown how this perspective has been used in classroom research. An alternative name for socio-cultural theory is 'socio-historical' theory, because (compared with other approaches to learning and development) it emphasizes that the development of human knowledge, collectively and individually, has a historical dimension. In this chapter, we will pursue this theme by looking at how time is used as a resource in dialogue, as teachers and learners talk and work together.

One of our specific interests will be in how the progress of classroom dialogue through time helps achieve educational outcomes. We will look at how classroom talk is used by teachers and learners to represent past shared experience, carry ideas forward from one occasion to another, approach future activities and achieve learning outcomes. Not all the seeds of knowledge that are sown in a classroom will grow, but we may be able to track some that do. Surprisingly, what might be called the *temporal dimension* of educational dialogue and interaction has not been given the attention it deserves, even by sociocultural researchers. Moreover, we believe that its study offers some very useful insights into the practical business of teaching and learning in schools.

Let us begin with a consideration of life in a primary (elementary) school. Each teacher and the members of a class usually stay together for the whole of a school year. Their classroom life is organized into lessons, which may be as short as half an hour or as long as two hours; but any one lesson usually represents part of a series dealing with a topic or a set of related topics, taking place at quite regular intervals. Although the efforts of the teacher and students in each lesson may be focused on specific goals, there is a cumulative quality to the educational process. Particular tasks will be set in the context of an overarching curriculum, some topics will take more than one session to pursue and the achievement of some kinds of skills and understanding may be prerequisites for more advanced work. The treatment of topics and development of skills may be planned by teachers as a staged process.

The teacher and classroom researcher Douglas Barnes observed: 'Most learning does not happen suddenly: we do not one moment fail to understand something and the next moment grasp it entirely' (Barnes, 1992, p.123). We might add that changes in our understanding of particular topics or subjects are often associated with interaction with other people. Education is not simply a matter of an individual accumulating information; it involves the gradual induction by teachers of students into new perspectives on the world, the gradual development of new problem-solving skills in the context of schoolwork, and new ways of using language for representing knowledge and making sense of experience that must be used by students in speech and writing if they are to become part of their communicative and intellectual repertoires.

The significance of the passage of time for the functioning of classroom dialogue for the development of knowledge and understanding has been recognized by several classroom researchers (see, for example, Erickson, 1996; Cobb, 1999; Crook, 1999; Issroff, 1999; Littleton, 1999; Wells, 1999, chapter 3; Alexander, 2000, chapter 15; Lemke, 2001; Gibbons, 2002; Roth, 2001, 2005, 2006; Nystrand et al., 2003; Rasmussen, 2005). It is also implicitly recognized in the life of educational institutions. In British schools, at least, some of the most important assessment is designed to test students' cumulative, integrated understanding of a subject and not just their recall of specific items from discrete lessons. From a student's perspective, school work should ideally have a cohesive, cumulative quality in which specific activities and their goals can be seen to form part of a greater whole, as part of a purposeful educational journey.

Continuity of personnel and the linking of the content of lessons can be expected to provide some coherence to children's experience of classroom education. However, for all students some discontinuity and incoherence will be inevitable, caused by such factors as their absences from crucial lessons in a sequence, their difficulties in keeping up with the pace of activities, and the effects of lack of concentration, boredom and distractions of many kinds. No less important will be the ways in which, and the extent to which, teachers take account of students' need for coherence in their curriculum planning and teaching strategies. Bereiter (1997) has highlighted the problems that may be caused by teachers and students pursuing goals that are based on different implicit time frames. Alexander (2000), Crook (1999) and several other educational researchers have also argued that coherent knowledge and purposeful understanding will not naturally emerge for students from their continuous immersion in classroom life: it has to be pursued actively as a goal, through the use of appropriate teaching strategies. A sociocultural perspective encourages us to see that language is our prime tool for making collective sense of experience, and the extent to which students will perceive cohesion and coherence in their classroom work is likely to be heavily dependent on how dialogue mediates that activity. Talk with a teacher, and with other students, is perhaps the most important means for ensuring that a student's engagement in a series of activities contributes to their developing understanding of science, mathematics or any other subject as a whole. In order to understand how classroom education succeeds and fails as a process for developing students' knowledge and understanding, we therefore need to understand the temporal relationship between the organization of teaching-and-learning as a series of lessons and activities and how it is enacted through talk. To put it another way: as learning is a process that happens over time, and learning is mediated through dialogue, we need to study dialogue over time to understand how learning happens and why certain learning outcomes result. We may then see more clearly how the precious resource of the time that a teacher and a class spend together can be used to good effect in the pursuit of children's education, or how it may be squandered.

The systematic study of classroom talk and learning over an extended period of time is a difficult enterprise. Just gathering the relevant data requires the researcher's substantial commitment of their own time for continual recording and observation. There is relatively little guidance available for a researcher wishing to study the temporal dimension of classroom talk, but some useful advice has been provided by Gee and Green (1998) and Scott *et al.* (2006). Gee and Green describe one of the functions of talk as 'connection building', whereby intertextual links are made by speakers in their joint meaning-making. Following other researchers such as Bloome and Egan-Robertson (1993), they identify this as an important characteristic of classroom discourse and suggest that useful insights can be gained into how classroom talk functions by addressing such questions as:

What sorts of connections (intertextual ties) are proposed, recognized, acknowledged, and interactionally made to previous or future interactions (activity) and to texts, to other people, ideas, things, institutions and discourses outside the current interaction?

Which processes, practices and discourses do [speakers] draw on from previous events/situations to guide the actions in the current situation (e.g., text construction)?
(Gee and Green, 1998, p.141)

Scott *et al.*, reporting a study of talk in school science lessons, offer the following advice:

> To understand the purpose of a specific teaching activity in a sequence of lessons it is necessary to determine how this particular activity fits with the whole sequence. . . . [Our] analysis of the discourse of science lessons involves an iterative process of moving backwards and forwards through time, trying to make sense of the episodes as linked chains of interactions.
>
> (Scott *et al.*, 2006, p.626)

Also within an analysis of learning in science lessons, Roth (2006) offers the valuable insight that it is only by pursuing the trajectory of students' learning over time that an analyst can begin to recognize the potential significance of the apparent repetition of certain actions (such as procedures in a practical scientific investigation) as part of the learning process. The same act repeated cannot be assumed to be 'the same' act in repetition, because it builds historically on the earlier event. This insight applies as much, of course, to the consideration of utterances as of non-verbal actions.

In our own research, we have described some ways that teachers commonly refer to past events and how these are involved in the joint construction of knowledge with their students. For example, teachers commonly use *recaps* to summarize what they consider to be the most salient features of a past event for the current activity (Edwards and Mercer, 1987; Mercer, 1995). Recaps can be *literal,* when a teacher simply sums up what happens ('Last week, we began reading *Macbeth*') or *reconstructive,* the latter being where the teacher 'rewrites history', presenting a modified version of events that fits his/her current pedagogic concerns (as when we observed a teacher saying to students that in the previous lesson 'you made oxygen and saw how it ignites' when in fact many of them had failed to do so). Teachers also frequently use *elicitations* to prompt students' recall about past events (for example 'Who can tell me what they found out about the moon in the last lesson?'). It is common too for them to mark past shared experiences as significant and relevant by using '*we statements*' (as in 'Remember when we looked at the map of Italy?'). In those ways teachers invoke common knowledge and highlight the continuities of educational experience, trying to draw students into a shared, cumulative and progressive understanding of the activities in which they are engaged. As we saw in Chapter 5, Alexander (2004) has suggested that one indicator that teacher–student talk deserves to be called 'dialogic' is that the teacher uses talk to provide a cumulative, continuing, contextual frame to enable students' involvement with the new knowledge they are encountering.

Into the classroom

To give our consideration of the temporal dimension a more solid base, we will next use examples of dialogue from a series of lessons in one primary classroom in south-east England. The first is Sequence 7.1 below. Please read it now and consider what sense you can make of the observed event from the transcript alone. All we will tell you at this stage is that the participants were a teacher and her usual class of 10- to 11-year-olds, and the extract is part of the recording that was made of an introductory whole-class session to a maths lesson. The children were sitting in groups of three or four at their tables, looking towards the teacher who was standing at the front of the class.

Sequence 7.1: Introductory whole-class plenary, 18 March

Teacher:	Before you go on to the next step on the computer what do you need to make sure that the whole group has done? Oh! More hands up than that. Emma?	
Emma:	Agreed.	
Teacher:	Agreed. The whole group needs to agree. OK, one of my speech bubbles. I wonder what kind of things we might hear each other saying during today's lesson?	*Teacher writes 'everybody agrees' on board. Teacher draws a speech bubble. Points to a child.*
Axel:	What do you think?	
Teacher:	What do you think? Anything else you might hear people saying as we have today's lesson? Kaye?	*Teacher writes 'What do you think?' in speech bubble.*
Kaye:	What is your idea?	*Teacher draws a speech bubble and writes in it 'What is your idea?'*
Teacher:	Brilliant! What's your idea? Oh, Sydney?	
Sydney:	Why do you think that?	
Teacher:	Excellent. Well done. Any other things we might hear people say? Rebecca?	*Teacher draws a speech bubble and writes 'Why do you think that?'*
Rebecca:	I'm not too sure on that idea. What do you think?	

Teacher:	Brilliant. Well done. What do we need to remember in our groups? Kiera?	*Teacher draws a new speech bubble.*
Kiera:	That everybody gets a turn to talk.	
Teacher:	Everybody gets a turn to talk.	*Teacher points to Anna.*
Anna:	Everybody needs to share their opinions.	
Teacher:	Yeah – and are we all the same?	
Children:	No.	
Teacher:	Will there be someone in your group that perhaps wants to talk all the time?	
Children:	Yes.	
Teacher:	Will there be someone in your group who doesn't want to talk at all?	
Class:	Yes!	
Teacher:	How are you going to get that person who doesn't want to talk at all to say something? Shane? What do you think? How are you going to get that person who sits there and doesn't say anything to say something in your group? Help him out Tyber.	
Tyber:	Ask them.	
Teacher:	Ask them – brilliant. What about that person who talks *all* the time?	*Emphasises 'all'.*
Alan:	Tell him to shut up.	
Teacher:	Ooh! Are you? I hope not, because that's not positive language is it? What could you do to help them out? Kiera?	
Kiera:	Ask them and then ask somebody else and then ask the other person.	*Teacher silences an interruption with a gesture.*
Teacher:	Brilliant. Making sure that you ask everybody in the group. Excellent. Kaye?	

We expect that readers could make a good deal of sense of what was going on in the observed lesson from the transcript. For those who have analysed classroom interaction, it would have many familiar linguistic features. (Our understanding of any example like this will itself have a temporal or historical quality, as we will draw on our past experience of any similar examples to make sense of the new one.) But to gain more than a superficial understanding of this sequence as an educational event, some additional background information is needed: and readers who had previously read

Chapters 5 and 6 will probably have drawn on that prior experience in making their interpretation of what was going on in Sequence 7.1. The talk came from a classroom involved in the *Thinking Together* research, being recorded during the project called Study 2 in Chapter 6, which was focused on the development of children's use of spoken language as a tool for reasoning in science and mathematics. The recording was made in one of our target classes, in which the teachers worked with members of the research team to set up a programme of activities for raising the children's awareness of how they talked and worked in groups. This was the sixth in a series of lessons in which the use of talk for reasoning had been given special attention. In the previous one (which we also recorded), she had discussed with children how they could most effectively work together to solve problems, drawing on the concept of exploratory talk as discussed in Chapter 5. (To recap: exploratory talk is discussion in which partners engage critically but constructively with each other's ideas; relevant information is offered for joint consideration; proposals may be challenged and counter-challenged, but if so reasons are given and alternatives are offered; agreement is sought as a basis for joint progress; and knowledge is made publicly accountable and reasoning is visible in the talk.)

In the lesson previous to that of Sequence 7.1, the teacher had drawn out from her discussion with her class the following three points, writing them up on the board as she did so:

1   Members of groups should seek agreement before making decisions.
2   Group members should ask each other for their ideas and opinions ('What do you think?').
3   Group members should give reasons for their views, and be asked for them if appropriate ('Why do you think that?').

She then put up on the wall of the classroom a set of ground rules for talk (as we explained in Chapter 5, this notion of ground rules, like that of exploratory talk, is a key element of the *Thinking Together* programme). These rules were as follows:

Our ground rules for talk
We share our ideas and listen to one another.
We talk one at a time.
We respect each other's opinions.
We give reasons to explain our ideas.
If we disagree we try to ask 'why?'
We always try to agree at the end.

As researchers we knew that the teacher had set two types of learning objectives for this lesson, one concerned with the study of mathematics and the other with encouraging the use of exploratory talk. Immediately after this introductory session, the children began to work on maths problems together in small groups, using a computer program called 'Function Machine'. Their maths objective was to work out how to solve the problem of what function had been applied to each number they put in to the 'machine', by considering the number that it produced as an output. The specific talk objective was to use the ground rules in doing this task, related to the broader objective (pursued over a series of lessons) of developing skills for effective collaboration. Just before the start of Sequence 7.1, the teacher had written both objectives on the board and explained them.

As the background information above explains, members of the research team had been involved in the planning that generated the educational content for this extract. This meant that the researchers were involved in its history and so, rather unusually, we could draw on past experience shared with the teacher when making sense of what was said and done. We were thus able to infer that in her talk the teacher is drawing directly upon prior experience shared with her class. She uses questions to draw out from the children not only relevant comments on how they should interact, but also a collective recall of previous lessons – most specifically, to establish a shared understanding of the ground rules for talk. We can see her characteristic teacher's use of 'we' in this respect: 'What do we need to remember in our groups?' She elicits *models of speech acts* that would represent an appropriate use of the ground rules they have agreed: the phrases 'What do you think?' 'Why do you think that?' which had been identified. She then encodes these models in the more permanent language mode of writing (her 'speech bubbles'), which could then travel through time as a shared resource for the class as they pursued their activity.

Several of the teacher's questions signify temporality, for example:

> Before you go on to the next step on the computer what do you need to make sure that the whole group has done?

> I wonder what kind of things we might hear each other saying during today's lesson?

> Will there be someone in your group that perhaps wants to talk all the time?

These utterances seem designed to highlight for students the ways that knowledge gained in past activity can be used to anticipate future needs. This one extract therefore shows a teacher using talk to attempt to build the future of her students' educational experience on the foundations of their shared history. Before we leave Sequence 7.1, please note the teacher's remark, 'I hope not, because that's not positive language is it?', which we will return to later.

Classroom talk in its temporal context

To appreciate how classroom talk develops over time, we need a good understanding of how it works *in context*. 'Context' is a complex notion: it is both historical and dynamic. Historically, any spoken interaction, in the classroom or elsewhere, will be located within a particular institutional and cultural context. In school, for example, educational activities, curriculum assessments and lesson topics are set in the context of the school curriculum. Their existence and significance in classroom talk cannot be properly understood without taking account of that. Speakers' relationships also have histories. Things that are said may invoke knowledge from the joint past experience of those interacting (for example their recall of previous activities they have pursued together), or from the rather different kind of common knowledge that is available to people who have had similar, though separate, past experiences (for example, two people conversing who had at different times been students at the same school might assume much shared understanding of both the personalities of the teachers and the layout of the buildings, even if they had never met while studying there).

The *dynamic* aspect refers to the fact that conversations are not scripted – they are improvized. Speakers' contributions are contingent on what their partners say, and speakers will not usually know in advance exactly what they are going to say. A conversational interaction depends on the participants having some knowledge in common, that they can take for granted: and the basis of common knowledge upon which their shared understanding depends is constantly being developed as they interact. The nature of the shared, contextualizing knowledge being invoked in any dialogue is therefore potentially quite complex. It is in a state of flux, as immediate shared experiences and corresponding conversational content provide the resources for building the temporal foundations of future talk. A profound problem for researchers wishing to understand how language is used to jointly construct knowledge (and, indeed, with understanding how conversational communication works at all) is inferring what knowledge resources speakers are using. Speakers may make explicit references to shared past experience or other types of common knowledge, but they often invoke such historical, temporal resources only implicitly. Observable features of interactions are likely to have unobservable determinants in the histories of the individuals, groups and institutional systems involved (see Littleton, 1999). And as the educational researcher Lemke remarks, 'Time is not Galilean in such systems; the longer term, the nonproximate event, may be more relevant to the next move than the immediately preceding event' (2001, p.23). However, we can only deal with this phenomenon in a partial, limited fashion, by sampling dialogue over time and by drawing in our analysis on any resources of knowledge we share with the speakers.

We also need to take into account that educational dialogue in classrooms is a special type of language, a genre (or set of genres) whose distinctive, functional qualities we discussed in Chapter 4 and which have been so well described by generations of classroom researchers. As we mentioned earlier in this chapter, some characteristic features of that genre, such as teachers' recaps, are designed to invoke knowledge from the joint past experience of those interacting (i.e. their recall of previous activities they have pursued together).

To make educational sense of a particular sequence of classroom dialogue, then, it would help to know not only what happened within the interaction, but also what happened before it, what the participants were expecting to happen, and what they learned from it. That is, it would be useful to have information about:

1   *The shared history of the participants.* It helps to know whether a teacher and a class have worked together before, if there have been previous lessons on this topic, and if the students had encountered this particular kind of task before (and so could be expected by the teacher to have some relevant past experience). This can, and should, strongly influence an analyst's interpretation of the meaning and significance of utterances for the participants – for example regarding the function of questions in which the teacher appears to be seeking information from the learner (i.e., are these stimulated recall questions, or attempts to gauge the understanding of a learner with whom the teacher is unfamiliar?). Access to recordings of prior lessons could thus be a crucial resource. However, it is not a comprehensive history of an event or the shared experience of the participants that analysts need, but rather those aspects of shared knowledge that the participants treat as relevant to their current task and so invoke in their dialogue. For instance, in Extract 1, the teacher's question 'What do you need to make sure that the whole group has done?' would have a very different meaning for members of a class who have spent a previous lesson discussing what a group should do to work effectively, from those of a class which was just beginning to do so on this occasion. The very same question could, depending on the local history of the exchange, invoke very different kinds of responses from a student. This issue also relates to the next point.

2   *The temporal development of the dialogue.* We not only need background information about shared experience prior to the observed event, we also want information about the progress of the talk itself. A conversation is like a sophisticated type of dual-control (or multi-control) track-laying vehicle: its participating 'drivers' use the history of their encounter to

build the foundations for its future path as it proceeds. Conversations run on contextual tracks made of common knowledge.

In their classic study of classroom talk, Barnes and Todd explain how when a group of children are working together:

> meanings for what is going on in the conversation are constructed not from any one utterance on its own, but from cycles of utterances, perhaps over quite lengthy sections of the interaction. Now these cycles are not readily isolable: they adhere to the interaction between utterances, and the speaker-hearer's intentions for, and interpretation of, these utterances. When we analyze talk, what we are trying to do is to feel our way into the meanings the participants made for the interaction as it happened. But the meanings which the participants made were not stable. They were fluid and changing, built up out of the existing knowledge and expectations which they brought to the situation, along with their own implicit summary of what went on in the conversation, and their reaction to that summary. Meanings change in response to on-going events in the conversation, which lead to a reinterpretation of what has gone on so far.
>
> (Barnes and Todd, 1977, p.17)

This dynamic aspect of conversational interaction is what Gee (1999) calls its reflexivity. It is the historically cumulative, reflexive nature of conversation which requires 'explicitness' to be treated as a relative concept, because speakers need only be as explicit as is necessary for effective communication (as Grice, 1975, so elegantly explained). If people conversing share a relatively advanced understanding of a technical subject, much basic knowledge about it can be left implicit, even if the relevant knowledge has been gained quite separately by the participants. They also build joint semantic resources for implicit reference as they continue to interact. Of course, speakers do not necessarily get this right. Inappropriate judgements about what to make explicit are a common source of misunderstandings, in classrooms as in other settings. Attending to the temporal dimension may help us understand this problematic aspect of the joint construction of knowledge.

3   *The trajectory of the event.* As well as the history of the event, it would also help to have some information about how participants perceive its projected future. For example, do the participants know that they have up to an hour or so to spend together on the problem, or is this jointly perceived as a brief encounter? Is it a preparation for a formal test? Is there evidence of a shared perception of the trajectory amongst participants? Is there a shared understanding that this educational task is part of a longer educational journey, or is it a 'one-off' event?

4   *The educational outcomes of the event.* The goal of some research into language and social interaction may be no more than an understanding of the nature of the process observed. But for educational researchers, there is also usually an interest in the educational value of any teaching-and-learning interaction. We may want to know if there is evidence that any students have been educated as a result of the dialogue observed. We may also want to explain why participation in the same educational, discursive events has apparently led to different educational outcomes among students. One way of exploring this is to track back from observable outcomes through the history of those events.

Of course, as researchers we will never have all the information we might want for making a temporal analysis, but that does not justify ignoring the information we can obtain. We can make efforts to gain some of it by observing and recording series of events over time, rather than single events; by talking to the participants; and by gathering other kind of documentary data such as timetables, teachers' lesson plans, students' work and so on. To use this information effectively, we also need a clear conceptualization of educational dialogue as a temporal process.

Back to the classroom

We now return to the *Thinking Together* classroom that figured in Sequence 7.1. Sequence 7.2 (below) took place ten days later, on the next occasion when that class was recorded. Again, it is taken from a whole-class session at the start of a lesson, before the children began a group-based activity.

Sequence 7.2: Introductory whole-class plenary, 29 March

Teacher:	Can you remember what we had to sort in our science lesson?
Anna:	Food.
Teacher:	Food. Brilliant! We had to sort it into different categories didn't we? This time we're going to be sorting numbers. So that's our objective – sorting numbers.

Writes this objective on board.

I'm going to work with Donal and Alan today and in my group I've decided I'm going to sort the numbers by multiples of three, and I don't care what they think. What's the matter Maya?

Teacher takes on role of child with grumpy expression.

Maya:	You should, um, decide as a group.
Teacher:	Oh super. There's one of our ground rules already, 'Decide as a group'. OK. How am I going to do that? Because I want to sort my numbers by multiples of three. How am I going to make sure that we decide that as a group?
Kiera:	Ask them what they think. Also, when you ask what they think, don't turn your back on them because that's not positive body language.
Teacher:	You mentioned positive body language. What other type of language do we need to make sure is positive? Not just our body language – come on Sydney – join in please. What other sort of language do we need to make sure is positive?
Child:	The way we talk.
Teacher:	The way we talk! Am I going to say 'I'm going to sort these in multiples of three!'?
Child:	No.
Teacher:	Maya, what would you say if you were in my situation?
Maya:	Um, 'I want to sort them by multiples of three. What do you think about it?'
Teacher:	That would be a good thing to say. *(and then a little later . . .)*
Teacher:	OK, as I'm wandering around the classroom and looking and watching and listening to what you are doing, I wonder what sort of things I might hear you saying. Go on. Tell your partner one thing you might say. Bernice, can you tell Sydney? And . . . stop! Ready? Looking this way. Donal's group. Share one of the things I might hear you say.
Donal:	What do you think?

Writes 'Decide as a group' on board.

Teacher writes 'Ask them what they think'.

Children talk to each other.

Teacher:	What do *you* think? Brilliant – Emma?	*Emphasizes the word 'you' and writes. 'What do you think?' on board.*
Emma:	Why do you think that?	
Teacher:	Why do you think that? That's another good one, not just what but *why* do you think that? Brilliant.	*Writes 'Why do you think that?' on board.*

For anyone who has read Sequence 7.1, there is a familiar quality about the opening discussion of Sequence 7.2. As in Sequence 7.1, the teacher is beginning a plenary session by checking the students' recall of how they are expected to work in a group. She begins this session with an appeal to the children's memory of past activity, by making an intertextual link to earlier dialogue: 'Can you remember what we had to sort in our science lesson?'

This appeal is responded to accordingly by one of the students. We can see here an exemplification of both the historical aspect and the dynamic aspect of classroom talk, as participants draw on their shared past experience to build the contextual foundations for their continuing interaction. As we mentioned earlier, an elicitation of this kind is one of several dialogic tools teachers commonly use to try to help children see the continuity of educational experience and to encourage them to recall knowledge of past events that is relevant to current or future activity.

Back in the 1970s, the linguists Sinclair and Coulthard (1975) showed that spoken interactions between teachers and students typically have a three-part structure. First there is an Initiation, usually in the form of a question, from the teacher. This elicits a Response from a student, to which the teacher typically provides an evaluative Follow-up or feedback. This unit of classroom dialogue is thus commonly known as an 'IRF exchange', or simply an 'IRF'. Sequence 7.1 opens with a classic IRF exchange. The teacher uses the 'Follow-up' to repeat Anna's response ('Food') and provide positive feedback on it. She then recaps the previous activity: 'We had to sort it into different categories didn't we?' In contrast to that historical review, her next remark is future-orientated: 'This time we are going to be sorting numbers. So that's our objective – sorting numbers'. By invoking the generic category of action of 'sorting', she marks as similar two classroom activities (one past and one in the immediate future) that might have seemed quite disparate to the students. Drawing on such shared experiential resources a teacher can use dialogue to set up and maintain an Intermental Development Zone (IDZ, as discussed in Chapter 4) to support learning, enabling participants to take a shared perspective on a task and pursue common (or at least compatible) goals. In this way a teacher can help students see a series of activities as stages on a learning journey rather than as disconnected events.

Moving on, we can see that the teacher next makes a very different kind of statement: 'I'm going to work with Donal and Alan to-day and in my group I've decided I'm going to sort the numbers by multiples of three, and I don't care what they think.' She appears to be role-playing an awkward child, and at first sight this seems an unusual kind of teacher-talk. But we see that Maya responds in a way that the teacher treats as appropriate – the flow of the interaction is smoothly maintained. Maya's response 'You should, um, decide as a group' shows that she is familiar with the teacher's rhetorical strategy and understands its pedagogic function. Her response also shows that she realizes that this dramatic characterization is not a diversion from the current topic, but an illustration of a transgression of the ground rules – and so demands a critical comment. The fact that the teacher and student can go directly into this role-play, without any explicit introduction, illustrates particularly well the historically contextualized, reflexive nature of talk in classrooms. Both teacher and child have the requisite common, contextualizing knowledge to make the interaction work; and they do not need to make this knowledge explicit. The collaborative success of this bit of dialogue suggests that an IDZ is being maintained: both teacher and student are operating within a shared frame of reference that supports the pursuit of the problem set by the teacher.

Later in the sequence the teacher asks, 'How am I going to make sure that we decide that as a group?' Kiera's response, 'Ask them what they think', paraphrases what the teacher had written up in a speech bubble in the earlier lesson (and which is now included as a permanent notice about ground rules for talk on the classroom wall). Kiera then goes on to mention the need for 'positive body language'. The teacher picks this up and highlights '(an)other type of language' that 'we need to make sure is positive'. As earlier observers of this class, we can infer that a routine has been established for opening these lessons – an inference we can check against our recorded data. We also see here the use by a child of a term ('positive language') used by the teacher at the very end of Sequence 7.1. It is very likely that a child's use of such a special term has its source in the teacher's talk, and our historical data supports this interpretation. Next, we go to another introductory plenary, a month later. The teacher is asking the children for comments on how they will work together.

Sequence 7.3: Introductory whole-class plenary, 26 April

Teacher: What would happen if I didn't check everyone agrees with the idea? I wonder what would happen – Emma? (*her reply is inaudible*) Yes, you'd be dominating the group. You'd be making decisions that not everybody perhaps has had a chance to think through.

Luke:	Positive body language.
Teacher:	What was that one you just said? Positive body language. Brilliant. That's not something I'm going to hear is it? No – it's something I can see. How do I see positive body language Donal?
Donal:	Looking at people and then you can see if they are nodding.
Teacher:	If you are looking at somebody it's going to be much more polite and show more respect than if you've got your back to somebody when they are talking.

We see here again the use of the term 'positive body language', reappearing like an echo of lessons past. It is a special term, a piece of technical vocabulary for talking about talk as a topic of study, which provides evidence of the historical continuity of the dialogue in this class as a small educational community. This illustrates well how technical language is first used by teachers and then appropriated by students. Our analysis also shows that the talk in a classroom over a series of lessons can be considered simultaneously as a series of language events and as one cohesive text. The repetition of the term 'positive body language' is a *cohesive tie* (as the linguists Halliday and Hasan, 1976 use the term), a link between the language of particular lessons. A search for the word 'positive' in all the talk data for this class showed that there were just two instances of a child using the term collocated with the word 'language' – in Sequences 7.2 and 7.3, in whole class sessions. The teacher used it five times, always collocated with 'language', in two of the five recorded lessons. There was no recorded evidence of children taking up this expression and making active use of it in their groups without the teacher: though as reflection on ways of talking was not ever specified as part of such activity this is not surprising. However, Donal's explanation of the term suggests that its meaning is commonly understood. We therefore have some temporal evidence of this class developing, *through* educational dialogue, a shared vocabulary for talking *about* educational dialogue.

Talk amongst students in small groups

So far, we have only presented extracts from teacher-led, whole class sessions. The next three extracts all come from group activities in the same classroom and the same series of lessons, when students were working together in groups of three without the teacher. The first, Sequence 7.4, is from a group activity that directly followed Sequence 7.2, the introductory whole-class plenary. Three children are working together on mathematics problems in which they have been given a series of numbers with one of the series missing, and have to work out the missing number. At the point the sequence begins, they are starting a new problem. Alan is making the first guess at what the missing item might be.

Sequence 7.4: Group work, 29 March

Alan:	Four. What do you think?
Muj:	Yes, four.
Neeran:	Is fifteen a multiple of four? No, four fours are sixteen.
Alan:	Yes it is. No. No.
Muj:	No.
Alan:	Is nine?
Muj:	No.
Neeran:	Why do you think that?
Alan:	Because it goes four, eight then twelve, so it misses nine out.

In Sequence 7.4 we see Alan and Neeran asking 'What do you think?' and 'Why do you think that?' These are literal reproductions of the model questions put up on the board by the teacher in a previous lesson (as explained earlier) and provided by other children (Donal and Emma) as responses to the teacher in Sequence 7.2. It might be expected that such questions would be commonly heard in group activity in any primary classroom: they are, after all, no more than everyday phrases with everyday meanings. However, as we described in earlier chapters, classroom research has shown that such an expectation is not justified. The kind of dialogue we have called exploratory talk is rare and so are questions such as 'What do you think?', 'Why do you think that?' and 'Do you agree?' that are associated with it. Moreover, recordings of group activity we made in this same classroom prior to the introduction of the *Thinking Together* programme showed little exploratory talk taking place. It is therefore a reasonable inference that the children in Sequence 7.4 are following the ground rules for talk that were established around a month before. Alan and Neeran's questions illustrate what we have called the historical context of dialogue: they reflect the shared past experience of the class. This gives them a different meaning than if they were uttered in another class where no special preparation for interthinking in groups had taken place. The questions serve not only to carry forward the discussion, but also as appeal to the agreed norms for behaviour within this community. In that sense the ground rules have shaped the talk dynamically, because they provide a basis for the talk to be carried along in a certain way. The talk embodies prior learning by the children about the use of language as a tool for thinking and learning together, and can also be seen to embody the teacher's objectives for this series of lessons for developing effective collaboration in groups. We are given a glimpse of the dialogic trajectory of activity in this class. An analysis of educational dialogue that took no account of the temporal dimension, with its historical and dynamic aspects of context, could provide only a relatively impoverished understanding of what was going on in Sequence 7.4.

It would have little useful to say about what learning was expected of the children and what had been learned.

The next two transcripts are from the activity of two different groups in the same class. Sequence 7.5 was recorded almost a month after Sequence 7.4; and the final example, Sequence 7.6, was recorded slightly more than a month after that. In both cases the children are involved in solving a maths problem in which they have to select an appropriate number to enter in a computer-based calculation.

Sequence 7.5: Group work, 26 April

Kylie:	Let's just try a smaller number. Who agrees we try a smaller number? I agree. (*Tony and Maya raise their hands*)
Rebecca:	I don't.
Kylie:	So – what number? Maya, you choose a number.
Maya:	Six.
Kylie:	Do we all agree on six? Tony and Maya? Yes Rebecca?
Rebecca:	No, try that other one.
Kylie:	We are! Do you agree on six?
Rebecca:	No.
Kylie:	Why?

Sequence 7.6: Group work, 7 June

Sofia:	Five, seven and five equals twelve. So put five.
Beau:	Do you agree?
Kirsty:	Yes, and then we need to sort this out.
	(*and then a little later . . .*)
Sofia:	I know, why don't we use the seven again?
Kirsty:	What do we do now?
Sofia:	What do you think we should do?
Kirsty:	I don't know, it's too hard. I have never done this before.
Beau:	I haven't done this before.
Sofia:	What can we remember? A blank square. All I can remember is numbers. Eight add one is nine.

In Sequences 7.5 and 7.6 we again see children using questions such as 'What do you think?' and 'Do you agree?', which can be traced directly back to the establishment of the ground rules in their class (by now several months earlier). We can also see them use other related but different expressions: 'Who agrees we try a smaller number?', 'What do we do now?' and 'What can we remember?' These can be read as evidence that they have not followed the ground rules only in a mechanistic way, by simply 'parroting' the model speech acts offered by the teacher, but rather have learned how to apply them in an appropriate, creative way in their discussions. In Sequence 7.6, Sofia's final remark 'What can we remember?' is interesting in itself, from a temporal perspective, because it is an appeal to the relevant shared knowledge of her group gained through earlier classroom activities, which might allow them to 're-cognize' (as Roth, 2006, puts it) the apparently new problem they are facing.

Summary

By examining their talk in its historical context, we can see that the children's discussion in Sequences 7.5 and 7.6 has been shaped by past events, namely the whole class and small group sessions of the *Thinking Together* lessons in which their teacher established the ground rules and guided the development of their skills in using language as a tool for reasoning. By examining both the process and the outcomes of the talk amongst teachers and children over time, it is possible to draw more valid and useful conclusions about the educational functions of dialogue than if the analysis is focused only on processes (as is often the case in sociolinguistic research and conversation analysis) or on outcomes (as is often the case in more psychological, experimental-style investigations – for more detail on methodological approaches, see Mercer *et al.*, 2004; Mercer, 2005). In this particular case, the temporal analysis of talk played a crucial role, when used in complement with the other types of analysis and measures described in Chapter 6, in evaluating the *Thinking Together* approach. In this way see how, over time, teachers can help the development of children's use of language as a cultural and cognitive tool.

Chapter 8

Some conclusions

In our consideration of dialogue and children's intellectual development, we have had in mind current debates about the role of educational research. Some have argued that researchers need to stand apart from practical concerns, maintaining a detached, critical stance as they strive to achieve a theoretically robust account of the processes and practices of education. In this case, the questions to be addressed would be those set by the researchers. Others have argued that the main aim and function of educational research should be to provide a strong evidence base to inform and guide educational practice. In this case, the research questions would need to be defined in collaboration with teachers, policy makers and others directly concerned with the quality of education.

We hope to have shown that applied, practical educational research can be simultaneously theoretical and practical. Indeed, we would argue that it is necessary to weave these two strands together. Theoretically informed ideas about teaching and learning, and hypotheses about the relationship between cognitive development and language use, can be transformed into empirical investigations; investigations that can then provide new insights into 'what works' and thus provide an evidential base for practice of the most robust kind. Applied studies can of course also result in the refinement, re-working and development of theory: and by 'theory' we do not mean some abstract, academic speculation (as it is often represented in the popular press) but rather an explanatory account that helps us understand the generalities of a phenomenon across specific situations and can be tested against the evidence provided by careful research.

Although we have not made it the subject of much explicit discussion, we hope also to have shown that we believe the most valuable and ethically defensible educational research is that which incorporates not only the concerns of researchers, but also those of teachers, policy makers and students too. It is our belief that researchers should undertake work *with* other education professionals and students, rather than conducting research *on* them, thereby recognising them as people with concerns rather than treating them as objects of concern.

In this final chapter we will sum up the main implications of our exploration of dialogue and development. First we will consider some issues related mainly to research and educational theory; and then we will turn to educational practice.

What can we conclude about the role of dialogue in the processes of learning and development?

As we explained in Chapter 6, giving children specific guidance in how to use language to reason together impacts positively on their collective problem-solving and curriculum learning. We have shown that it enhances their individual performance scores on a non-verbal test of reasoning too, and this has particular relevance to the validity of a sociocultural theory of education. The research findings we have described support Vygotsky's claim that, through the mediation of the cultural tool of language, social interaction shapes intellectual development. We have shown that through engaging in collective thinking, children learn how to think better on their own. Note that this is not the same as saying that thought is shaped by language, or making any similar broad, deterministic statement. There are many influences on children's developing intellect, some of which may not be linguistically mediated or even socially mediated; and children may take part in a great many dialogues that have no significant influence on how they think. But that is not a problem for sociocultural theory, or for those of us wishing to apply it to the study of education, because we are not concerned with the effects of interaction in general. Rather, we are interested in the effects of specific kinds of interactions – and in our case those associated with the processes of dialogic teaching and exploratory talk. On that basis, we are able to say 'Vygotsky was right!'

A question then arises: what exactly is the influential effect that we have recorded? Can we provide a more specific psychological explanation than saying that engagement in reasoned dialogue improves individual children's reasoning? We can, but only by offering two possible types of explanation. We might call them the 'learning' explanation and the 'development' one. Remember that all the children involved in our projects, both in target and control classes, had experience of tackling the Raven's test in groups before they attempted it (in another version) as a solitary exercise. Our evidence shows that the target children also improved their *collective* performance on this group exercise significantly more than the control children. The learning explanation of why the target children became better at solving the Raven's problems over the duration of the project would be as follows. Through their *Thinking Together* experience they had learned how to inter-think effectively, and so were regularly sharing good strategies for doing the test amongst the members of the group, constructing new strategies together, critically examining any strategies group members proposed and delaying making decisions until the group members were all satisfied with the final decision. The control children did not work as such effective teams. When the target children came to do the test individually, they had access to the problem-solving strategies that had been used and developed in their group, especially because those strategies and the reasoning underpinning them would have been made explicit. They would therefore have access to more and better strategies than the control children, and so would perform better. This explanation means that dialogue is certainly good for learning. It would also be supported by our evidence that target children also improve their attainment in mathematics, science and English. For some children, too, learning to collaborate is itself a major achievement.

The development explanation is that the target children had not simply picked up more useful strategies from their group problem-solving sessions, they had become more dialogic thinkers. That is, they had appropriated the ground rules of exploratory talk so that they became more able to hold a kind of reasoned intramental discussion. To a greater extent than the control children, they had acquired the procedures of rational thinking, which include considering all reasonable alternatives and making a relatively detached, critical examination of their plans before acting. This is a more daring explanation because it links rational thought with rational dialogue, not merely in some analogical or metaphorical way, but in an epistemological way.

Our colleague Rupert Wegerif has suggested that the learning explanation is essentially that promoting exploratory talk enables the opening and maintaining of a dialogic space of reflection in which children can jointly pursue creative solutions to problems (Wegerif, in press (b)), which would seem a worthwhile outcome in its own right. It may be that both of these explanations, the learning and the development explanations, have some validity: they are not mutually exclusive. In any case, the design of our studies and the kind of data we gathered does not allow us to choose between them. There are ways that this issue could be pursued through future research, and it may be that we will do so. But on the basis of either explanation, we now have good reasons to assert the value of dialogue, of a certain nature and content, for children's intellectual development. There is no absolute need to distinguish between these explanations before adopting a sociocultural theoretical perspective, or using the results we have described as a basis for improving educational practice.

On the basis of the *Thinking Together* research we have shown that through collectively (re)constructing and negotiating ground rules for talk and interacting that embody and enact the ground rules for exploratory talk, children and their teachers are actively configuring and reconfiguring a distinctive, inclusive, flexible environment for working together. Children talking in an exploratory way in their group are simultaneously:

- creating a positive climate of trust and a culture of collaboration;
- opening up and maintaining a dialogic space for pursuing creative solutions to problems;
- being inducted into culturally valued, useful ways of using language to get things done; and
- learning ways of reasoning that they can take away and use on their own.

Some implications for research on dialogue, learning and development

One of our main aims has been to show that dialogue deserves to be given not only a more visible, explicit role in accounts of how children learn and develop through their educational experience, but that these accounts need to be more closely related to the nature and uses of talk as it happens in classrooms. In much research on the processes of teaching, learning and cognitive development, there has been little recognition that these three elements are connected by dialogue. Strange as it may seem to anyone involved in education, there is a long-established line of experimentally based psychological research on the processes and theory of learning that has taken no account of the processes of teaching. The same could be said, with recent exceptions, for the study of children's cognitive development, in that the study of children's cognitive development was kept separate from the study of the social worlds of childhood. There has even been considerable research on teaching, sometimes under the headings of didactics and pedagogy, that has given little attention to the active role of learners, to what they achieve from their participation in encounters with teachers or from their interactions in the classroom with each other. As the study of all such matters is increasingly integrated, we are sure we are not alone in believing that the time has now come to develop a unifying sociocultural, dialogic theory of how knowledge is jointly constructed and how learners achieve greater understanding.

One obvious aspect of this theory-building must involve relating accounts of teacher–student interaction to those about interactions amongst students. We can begin to address this by considering two concepts that have figured largely in earlier chapters: 'dialogic teaching' and 'exploratory talk'. The first, in the sense it has been introduced by Robin Alexander (2004), is essentially a specification of good practice, derived from both research on the nature of dialogue and observations of talk in primary classrooms across a range of cultural settings. It has clear links, in both its origins and its nature, with some other concepts devised by educational researchers, such as 'reciprocal teaching' (Brown and Palincsar, 1989), contingent tutoring (Wood and Wood, 1999), 'dialogic enquiry' (Wells, 1999) 'dialogic spells' (Nystrand et al., 2003). We also related it to Mortimer and Scott's (2003) examination of science teaching, using their matrix of dialogic/interactive/ authoritative teaching strategies.

As an educational concept, dialogic teaching is both descriptive and prescriptive. It represents an approach to classroom teaching that 'aims to be more consistently searching and more genuinely reciprocal and cumulative' (Alexander, 2004, p.1) than is usually observed in classrooms, around the world. It requires a teacher to orientate to the state of understanding of students, engage them in exchanges that will reveal the changing limits and possibilities of their developing interests and understandings, and adjust their communication strategies accordingly as classroom interaction progresses. It involves students taking an active, engaged role in both their own learning and that of their classmates; becoming explicitly part of a collective endeavour. It requires the creation and maintenance of the kind of dynamic intersubjectivity we have called an Intermental Development Zone.

Although derived from the study of children's talk in groups without a teacher present, the notion of exploratory talk shares some of the characteristics of the type of teacher–student communication that Mortimer and Scott call 'dialogic/interactive'. The concept of exploratory talk typifies interaction that depends on the creation, monitoring and adaptation of a dynamic state of intersubjectivity – Wegerif's dialogic space – in which ideas can be publicly considered, examined, tested and employed in a way that avoids the individualistic and competitive qualities of the kind of interaction we have typified as disputational talk. It is talk designed for the pursuit of common tasks, the sharing of relevant knowledge, the joint construction of new knowledge and the improvement of understanding. A teacher involved in a dialogic/interactive episode with a whole class could be considered to be orchestrating exploratory talk.

An additional link that might be made between teacher–student and student–student interaction can be made through the concept of scaffolding. As you may remember from Chapter 2, Wood et al. (1976) first introduced this idea as a metaphor to capture the way in which an expert tutor (such as a parent) can support a young child's progress through a complex task. They described six functions of the tutor in scaffolding:

1   To orientate the child's attention to the version of the task defined by the tutor.
2   To reduce the number of steps that are required to solve a problem, thus simplifying the situation in a way that the learner can handle the components of the process.
3   To maintain the activity of the child as she/he strives to achieve a specific goal, motivating him/her and directing her/his actions.
4   To highlight critical features of the task for the learner.

5   To control the frustration of the child and the risk of failure.
6   To provide the child with idealized models of required actions.

In educational research, this metaphor has inevitably been used to describe the involvement of a teacher with students. Sometimes, as we argued earlier, it tends to be used too loosely, as merely an educational jargon synonym for 'help': but it still has value and should not be abandoned. Our view is that, if defined operationally and used with restraint, it has great value for understanding teacher–student interactions (as shown, for example, by its application in the language classroom by Gibbons, 2002 and others). Moreover, it can also be adapted to understand the processes of collaborative learning, suggesting that scaffolding can occur between peers working together on a task or a problem. As reported in Fernández *et al.* (2001/2002), an analysis of the talk of children solving problems together has shown that all the scaffolding functions ascribed to tutors by Wood *et al.* (1976) can be found in children's talk in *Thinking Together* groups – though this does not necessarily imply an intentional guiding role on the part of participants. Children may not be consciously trying to scaffold the development of each other's understanding (as might a teacher), but the ground rules of exploratory talk that they are following have this effect anyway.

As will be clear from the transcribed examples in Chapters 5, 6 and 7, children use exploratory talk to orientate collectively to the parameters of the task they are working on, sharing ideas as to how best to approach it. Thus the first scaffolding function, of orientating and defining, can also be enacted in the symmetrical talk of children. In terms of the second function, it is evident that through their exploratory talk together children can share different perspectives on a problem, which helps them break it down into its components, making the task of understanding easier for each individual child. Function 3 underscores the importance of encouragement, motivation and maintaining children's on-task activity.

The comparisons of pre- and post-intervention talk presented in Chapter 6 indicate that, having being inducted into exploratory ways of talking and relating, children engage in more sustained episodes of talk and joint activity when working together to solve problems. They appear to be more motivated to collaborate to reach agreed solutions – because they motivate each other. Whereas a teacher might explicitly plan to highlight the critical features of a problem to help children understand it (Function 4), in more symmetrical talk activities these features often emerge in an unplanned way as children share understandings and explain solutions as they work together. We have seen instances where a learner highlights critical aspects of a problem that contribute to the group's solving of the problem.

Working in a group also can mean that both risk and frustration are shared and therefore can be reduced for any individual. When children are talking disputationally, failure to solve the problem is often blamed on an individual. However, an essential ground rule of exploratory talk is that responsibility is shared, and this sharing serves to reduce individual risk and any sense of frustration. Thus the fifth scaffolding function can also be seen in talk amongst peers.

The sixth, and final, function relates to the provision of idealized models of required actions. This is often found at the point where one member of the group has to explain to another how a solution was achieved. In this way, group members support each other and so travel further in an intellectual sense than they would by using other types of talk or when working alone.

Whilst the metaphor of scaffolding has helped us understand the ways in which language can enable joint thinking and learning, this concept can only take us so far. The metaphor implies a temporary support that is removed once the construction work has been completed. But language is not merely used to provide temporary support for collective thinking: there is no stage after which it is no longer required. It is the very means by which people think and learn together. In conflict with the notion of scaffolding, language supports learning in ways that are dialogic, dynamic and continuous, maintained by the responsive and reciprocal ways in which participants use it.

In Chapter 7, we used data from one of our interventional classroom research projects, but not to support Vygotsky's claims or to present evidence for the effectiveness of the *Thinking Together* programme. Rather, we used the data to support our own claim that the relationship between time, talk and learning is intrinsically important to classroom education, and deserves more attention by those responsible for both research and practice. The coherence of educational experience is dependent on talk amongst participants, and so analyses of the ways that their continuing shared experience is represented and the ways that talk itself develops and coheres over an extended period are required if we are to understand the process of teaching-and-learning.

Concepts such as reflexivity, intertextuality and the Intermental Development Zone, as discussed earlier, can be used to highlight the dialogic, dynamic, self-contextualizing nature of classroom talk. In broader terms, a sociocultural perspective provides an appropriate theoretical base for developing a more temporally sensitive understanding of teaching and learning. But stronger conceptual links need to be built between the different levels of human activity identified by sociocultural theory – the cultural, the psychological and the social – so that we do not treat the cultural context of educational activity as static and given, but explain how it is constituted, renewed and transformed through the creative activities of people in conversation and embodied in the products of joint intellectual endeavour. We need to take account of what Lemke has called the multiple timescales of human social activity, development and learning, so that we are 'as willing to look at biography and history as at situations and moments, as methodologically and theoretically prepared to study institutions and communities as to study students and classrooms' (2001, p.25).

Methodologically, there is no doubt that we need better ways of analysing classroom talk as a continuing, social mode of thinking, which represent the ways in which the joint construction of knowledge is negotiated, contested, resourced and achieved over time. Talk that mediates continuing joint intellectual activity poses a considerable methodological challenge for a discourse analyst because of its reflexivity. In Chapter 7 we suggested that every conversational interaction has a historical aspect and a dynamic aspect. Historically, the interaction is located within a particular institutional and cultural context, and speakers' relationships also have local and more specific histories. Speakers may invoke any knowledge from the past experience of all those interacting, whether gained separately or jointly. The dynamic aspect refers to the fact that talk is inherently reflexive: its contextual base is in a constant state of flux, as immediate shared experiences and corresponding conversational content provide the resources for building future conversational context. A key problem for researchers concerned with explaining how talk is used for the joint construction of knowledge (or, indeed, with understanding how conversational communication functions at all) is understanding how speakers build contextual foundations for their talk.

We can only examine this in a partial, limited fashion, by sampling their discourse over time and by drawing in our analysis on any resources of common knowledge we share with the speakers. Understanding the creation of shared knowledge over extended periods of time will bring with it many other challenges for researchers. For example, as learners establish a shared history and develop common knowledge, the need to be verbally explicit about their work declines. For the participants in a collaboration, this is undoubtedly an asset. For researchers of productive interaction, however, this backgrounding is an analytic challenge. But however difficult it may be to find solutions, the problems cannot be avoided. We need to find ways of representing how the joint construction of knowledge is achieved by participants over time, because the process of teaching-and-learning depends on the development of a foundation of common knowledge.

A temporal analysis can help us see how students' ideas change through the extended process of interaction with a teacher and each other and how new concepts, ways of using language and ways of solving problems are appropriated. Although our focus has been on talk, our argument for the significance of the temporal dimension in the study of educational events and processes has a wider relevance, with implications for the kind of information we need to gather. If, as researchers, we want to appreciate the educational value of an observed interaction between a teacher and a class of students, we should seek available information about what happened before that interaction and what happened subsequently. It would also be helpful to know what the participants expected from the event and to make some assessment of what the students learned from it. This is no more than common sense, but it is nevertheless not consistent with some research methodologies. Analytic methods that do not recognize or deal with the temporal development of talk, its reflexivity and cohesive nature over longer timescales than one episode or lesson will inevitably fail to capture the essence of the educational process. Methods for analysing discourse in which the analyst only attends to the relationship between contributions made by participants in one recorded conversation, without applying available information about previous related interactions and historically contextual knowledge shared by participants (as seems to have been advocated by some conversation analysts, for example Heritage, 1984; Schegloff, 1992, 1997) would simply not work. Other researchers making functional analyses of language in institutional settings, including those outside education, have made this point (for example Hester and Francis, 2000; Makitalo and Säljö, 2002). The use of coding schemes in which utterances with the same syntactic form and/or explicit content are taken to have the same pragmatic or semantic value, regardless of their location in the temporal sequence of communication, would also be inappropriate for addressing the kinds of questions with which we have been concerned. Rather than trying, in the interests of objectivity, to distance ourselves as analysts from the perspectives of participants in the long conversations of teaching and learning, we would rather try to share their perspectives. As Roth (2001) says, in advocating the dual role of teacher-researcher, knowing a school culture from the inside allows researchers to appropriate participants' competence systems and so enables a richer interpretation of observed language and events.

Teachers use talk to sow seeds from which, in time, may grow the understanding of their students. Dialogues with teachers, and with each other, enable students to consolidate and develop their understanding over time, so that they can build new understanding upon the foundations of past experience. As educational researchers, we need to understand more about the temporal processes and outcomes of educational dialogues, because only then will we be able to help teachers see more clearly how the precious resource of the time spent with their students can be used to best effect.

Some implications for educational practice

What life skills do we hope that children gain from education? One might be the ability to communicate and work well with other people; and another might be the ability to think and learn effectively alone. To most people, these may seem very different kinds of abilities, not least because the first is social and the second is solitary. But in this book we have shown that they are closely linked. The *Thinking Together* research has shown how a well-designed programme of language-based classroom activities can make an important contribution to the development not only of children's language and communication skills, but also to their reasoning and learning. We have also explained that teachers play a crucial part in this process, enabling children to participate in the renewal of culture and not just its reproduction. Other research, beyond our own, supports these conclusions.

It is important to realize that our argument is not that children, or students of any age, should be encouraged to adopt strange, uncomfortable ways with words. Rather, we are arguing that education should provide children with a kind of understanding about the power of language that will allow them to choose to use it as they see fit, in ways that are fit for purpose. The nature and value of exploratory talk is appreciated, albeit implicitly, by many people, perhaps most. Yet it remains an elusive occurrence in many encounters when it would be a useful tool (and not only in school, or amongst children). Most of the time, classroom recordings capture discussions in which children don't listen to each other, in which one person dominates the proceedings, in which they argue unproductively, or in which participants seem happy to go along with whatever anyone says without any reflection or debate. So there is an apparent paradox: teachers, and many other people, are able to specify what constitutes a good discussion, but such discussions occur very rarely in most classrooms. Why should this be so? As we suggested in Chapter 5, one likely reason is that teachers of students of all ages often assume that students will know how to talk and work together and so rarely give them explicit instructions or guidance in how to make a good discussion happen. Instead, teachers rely on students' out-of-school language experience to provide them with strategies for thinking together. But if that experience does not include much reasoned discussion, students may not understand the value of that particular language genre, or know the communicative strategies involved.

For some children, then, school may provide the only real opportunity for engaging in focused, reasoned discussion and so developing important language and thinking skills. As Barnes and Todd put it so well in the conclusion to their own study of talk in groups: 'If schooling is to develop in young people the qualities needed for responsible adult life, such learning has an important place in the repertoire of the social relationships teachers have at their disposal' (1995, p.166). As they also conclude, the solution will require a careful balance of teacher-led and group-based activity, with the latter giving children opportunities to take some responsibility for their own learning and development.

The research we have described in this book demonstrates the importance of teachers providing guidance for children's collaborative activity, and doing so in three main ways:

1 They should take an active role in guiding their pupils' use of language and modelling ways it can be used for thinking collectively. Teachers should ask children to give reasons to support their views, engage them in extended discussions of topics, and encourage them to see that responding need not simply mean providing the 'right' answer. The aim should be to create, to an extent that would be unusual in most classrooms today, more of the kinds of interactions that are indicative of dialogic teaching.

2 Teachers should establish an appropriate set of ground rules for talk in class, building on children's own raised awareness of how language can be used so that the children treat the ground rules as their own. These rules should become part of the common knowledge of the class, to be invoked in all relevant activity.

3 They must ensure that curriculum-related group activities are well-designed to elicit debate and joint reasoning. Not all joint activities require much reasoning: only those that do will provide the kind of impetus that is required for learning and development. The best activities will stretch the joint intellectual resources of a group to the extent of their pooled knowledge and understanding, but be ultimately achievable.

There are also implications for the design of curricula, the degrees of freedom allowed to teachers in pursuing the needs of their students and the ways schools and governments assess teaching, learning and development.

There is certainly much more to discover about the ways that language experience in the classroom can contribute to the development of children's abilities to communicate, learn and reason, but what is known now provides a well-informed basis for the creation of a more dialogic, and more effective, educational practice. It is an uncontroversial claim that, through social interaction, children learn how language can be used to describe the world, to make sense of life's experience and to get things done. However, we have shown that what children learn from talk in the classroom, and how significant it is for their psychological development and educational progress, will depend a great deal on the range and quality of the dialogues in which they engage. It is important to recognize and celebrate the diversity of children's language experience outside school, but it is also crucial to recognize that different social environments will not necessarily provide the same range of language experiences. As we argued in Chapter 6, confusion about the ways language varies in relation to social and functional factors has hindered the proper consideration of what schools should offer children as guidance in using the cultural and psychological tool of language. There is no research evidence to persuade us that all children, in the crucial years of their development, naturally encounter all the language genres that they might need for taking responsible control over their own lives: but there is evidence to the contrary. Good teaching can make a world of difference to children's futures. Without guidance, instruction and encouragement from a teacher, many children may not gain access to some very useful ways of using language for reasoning and working collaboratively, because those ways with words are simply not a common feature of the language of their out-of-school lives. This argument does not involve the denigration of the language habits of any community or sector of society, or the need for children to be encouraged to forsake those habits. But it does mean that education must provide children with opportunities for learning new and useful language-based ways of thinking. To do otherwise upholds an inequitable *status quo* and undermines the empowering potential of school-based education.

An example of a *Thinking Together* lesson

Lesson **Pet shop**
8

In the **Talk Box**	• Models or pictures of pets – as many as possible. • Worksheet 8a What do the pets need? • Worksheet 8b Pet shop people

Learning objectives

To give reasons, evaluate evidence and compare ideas.
To recognise relevant facts.

> We are using things we think are important to give reasons and to make choices.

Success criteria

> I can say which things are most important and why. I can share my ideas and try to reach agreement.

Whole class work I

Explan that the group are the owners of a pet shop. They have to make sure that people choose and take home a pet that will really suit them. If not, the animal may not be well treated. Invite children to choose a 'pet' from the Talk Box. Discuss with the class what each pet needs to be happy and healthy.

Ask the children to recall the Talk Box Rules.

Explain that they will be working in a group and should try to use the rules to think about each other's ideas, and to use the information to make their best decision.

Show and explain the learning objectives for this lesson.

Share the success criteria with the children.

Group work

The first discussion task is for the group to talk together to fill in Worksheet 8a, using ticks and crosses to indicate what they think each pet needs.
Ask them to ensure that they agree
on decisions.

The second task is to look at the people visiting the pet shop. Ask the groups to talk together to make decisions about which visitor should take which pet home. It is important to give reasons and for the group to think together to decide on the best reason.

Whole class work 2

Ask the groups to report and justify their choices.

Ask the children to comment on their group's use of the Talk Box Rules.

Was it easy or hard to use the rules? Were there any disagreements, and how were these sorted out? Should the rules be changed? Can anyone think of an example of a good reason given by a group mate? Who was a good listener? Who provided useful information (etc.)?

Which information about the people does *not* help you to decide?

(Picture cards include irrelevant information, for example whether there is a car, a mobile phone, a computer, etc.)

LESSON 8

Use the success criteria to discuss whether the learning objectives have been met.

Decide if the Talk Box Rules helped the groups to work together well. Should the rules be changed?

Extension activity: Follow up for individual reasoning

Ask the children to work individually to think about a particular pet they would really like to have ('I must have this pet because . . . !') Draw the pet. Record what it needs. Record reasons why they should be allowed to own this pet – as persuasively as possible.

Try to persuade a partner, group or adult that they should have this pet. Ask children to identify which were the most persuasive reasons.

	Guinea pig	Dog	Parrot	Kittens	Fish	Gerbil
Garden						
Lots of space						
A walk						
Food every day						
Cleaning out						
Vet						
Company						

Worksheet 8a Pet shop: What do the pets need?

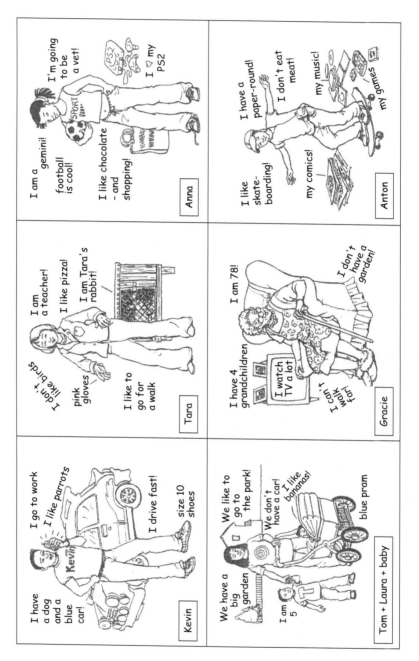

Anna

I am a gemini!

football is cool!

I like chocolate - and shopping!

I'm going to be a vet!

I ♡ my PS2

Tara

I am a teacher!

I like pizza!

I am Tara's rabbit!

I don't like birds

pink gloves

I like to go for a walk

Kevin

I have a dog and a blue car!

I go to work

I like parrots

I drive fast!

size 10 shoes

Anton

I have a paper-round!

I don't eat meat!

my music!

my games

I like skate-boarding!

my comics!

Gracie

I am 78!

I have 4 grandchildren

I watch TV a lot

I can't walk far!

I don't have a garden!

Tom + Laura + baby

We like to go to the park!

We don't have a car!

I like bananas!

blue pram

We have a big garden

I am 5

Worksheet 8b Pet shop people

References

Alexander, R. (2000) *Culture and Pedagogy: International Comparisons in Primary Education*, Oxford: Blackwell.

Alexander, R. (2004) *Towards Dialogic Teaching: Rethinking Classroom Talk*, Cambridge: Dialogos.

Alexander, R. (2005) 'Culture, dialogue and learning: Notes on an emerging pedagogy', paper presented at the *International Association for Cognitive Education and Psychology (IACEP)*, 10th International Conference, University of Durham, UK, July.

Anderson, R.C., Chinn, C., Waggoner, M. and Nguyen, K. (1998) 'Intellectually-stimulating story discussions', in J. Osborn and F. Lehr (eds) *Literacy for All: Issues in Teaching and Learning*, New York: Guilford Press.

Arvaja, M. (2005) 'Collaborative knowledge construction in authentic school contexts', doctoral thesis, Institute of Educational Research, University of Jyväskylä, Jyväskylä: University Printing House.

Azmitia, M. and Montgomery, R. (1993) 'Friendship, transactive dialogues and the development of scientific reasoning', *Social Development* 2 (3): 202–221.

Bakhtin, M. (1981) *The Dialogic Imagination*, Austin: University of Texas Press.

Barbieri, M. and Light, P. (1992) 'Interaction, gender and performance on a computer-based task', *Learning and Instruction* 2 (1): 199–213.

Barnes, D. (1976) *From Communication to Curriculum*, Harmondsworth: Penguin Books.

Barnes, D. (1992) 'The role of talk in learning', in K. Norman (ed.) *Thinking Voices: The Work of the National Oracy Project*, London: Hodder and Stoughton.

Barnes, D. and Todd, F. (1977) *Communication and Learning in Small Groups*, London: Routledge and Kegan Paul.

Barnes, D. and Todd, F. (1995) *Communication and Learning Revisited*, Portsmouth, NH: Heinemann.

Barron, B. (2000) 'Achieving co-ordination in collaborative problem-solving groups', *Journal of the Learning Sciences* 9 (4): 403–436.

Bennett, N. and Cass, A. (1988) 'The effects of group composition on group interactive processes and pupil understanding', *British Educational Research Journal* 15 (1): 19–32.

Bennett, N. and Dunne, E. (1992) *Managing Classroom Groups*, London: Simon and Schuster.

Bereiter, C. (1997) 'Situated cognition and how to overcome it', in D. Kirschner and J. Whitson (eds) *Situated Cognition: Social, Semiotic and Psychological Perspectives*, Hillsdale, NJ: Erlbaum.

Bernstein, B. (1971) *Class, Codes and Action Vol. I: Theoretical Studies Towards a Sociology of Language*, London: Routledge and Kegan Paul.

Bernstein, B. (1975) *Class, Codes and Action. Vol. III: Towards a Theory of Educational Transmissions*, London: Routledge and Kegan Paul.

Blatchford, P. and Kutnick, P. (2003) 'Developing groupwork in everyday classrooms', Special Issue, *International Journal of Educational Research*, 39 (1–2): 1–172.

Blatchford, P., Kutnick, P., Baines, E. and Galton, M. (2003) 'Towards a social pedagogy of classroom groupwork', *International Journal of Educational Research* 39: 153–172.

Blaye, A. (1988) 'Confrontation sociocognitive et resolution de probleme', unpublished doctoral thesis, University of Provence: Aix-en-Provence.

Bloome, D. and Egan-Robertson, A. (1993) 'The social construction of intertextuality and classroom reading and writing', *Reading Research Quarterly* 28 (4): 303–333.

Brown, A.L. and Palincsar, A.S. (1989) 'Guided, co-operative learning and individual knowledge acquisition', in L.B. Resnick (ed.) *Knowing, Learning and Instruction*, Hillsdale, NJ: Lawrence Erlbaum.

Bruner, J.S. (1978) 'The role of dialogue in language acquisition', in A. Sinclair, R. Jarvella and W. Levelt (eds) *The Child's Conception of Language*, New York: Springer-Verlag.

Bruner, J.S. (1985) 'Vygotsky: a historical and conceptual perspective', in J.V. Wertsch (ed.) *Culture, Communication and Cognition: Vygotskian Perspectives*, Cambridge: Cambridge University Press.

Chinn, C.F. and Anderson, R. (1998) 'The structure of discussions that promote reasoning', *Teachers College Record* 100: 315–368.

Claxton, G. (2002) 'Education for the learning age: a sociocultural approach to learning to learn', in G. Wells and G. Claxton (eds) *Learning for Life in the 21st Century*, Oxford: Blackwell.

Cobb, P. (1999) 'Individual and collective mathematical learning: the case of statistical data analysis', *Mathematical Thinking and Learning* 18 (1): 46–48.

Cobb, P., Yackel, K., and McClain, K. (2000) (eds) *Symbolizing and Communicating: Perspectives on Mathematical Discourse, Tools, and Instructional Design*, Mahwah, NJ: Erlbaum.

Cohen, E.G. (1994) 'Restructuring the classroom: conditions for productive small groups', *Review of Educational Research* 64 (1): 1–35.

Cook, G. (2003) *Applied Linguistics*, Oxford: Oxford University Press.

Crook, C. (1994) *Computers and the Collaborative Experience of Learning*, London and New York: Routledge.

Crook, C. (1999) 'Computers in the community of classrooms', in K. Littleton and P. Light (eds) *Learning with Computers: Analysing Productive Interaction*, London: Routledge.

Daniels, H. (2001) *Vygotsky and Pedagogy*, London: Routledge/Falmer.

Davis, A. (1991) 'Piaget, teachers and education: into the 1990s', in P. Light, S. Sheldon and M. Woodhead (eds) *Learning to Think*, London: Routledge.

Dawes, L. (2004) 'Talk and learning in classroom science', *International Journal of Science Education* 26 (6): 677–695.

Dawes, L. (2005) 'Speaking, listening and thinking with computers', in L. Grugeon, L. Dawes, L. C. Smith and L. Hubbard (eds) *Teaching, Speaking and Listening in the Primary School (Third Edition)*, London: David Fulton.

Dawes, L. and Sams, C. (2004a) 'Developing the capacity to collaborate', in K. Littleton, D. Miell and D. Faulkner (eds) *Learning to Collaborate, Collaborating to Learn*, New York: Nova.

Dawes, L. and Sams, C. (2004b) *Talk Box: Speaking and Listening Activities for Learning at Key Stage 1*, London: David Fulton.

Dawes, L., Mercer, N. and Wegerif, R. (2003) *Thinking Together: A Programme of Activities for Developing Speaking, Listening and Thinking Skills for Children aged 8–11*, Birmingham: Imaginative Minds Ltd.

Dawes, L., English, J., Holmwood, R., Giles, J., and Mercer, N. (2005) *Thinking Together in Geography: Using Speaking and Listening to Develop Thinking Skills at KS3*, Stevenage: Badger Publishing.

DES (Department of Education and Science) (1975) *The Bullock Report*, London: HMSO.

DFE (Department for Education) (1995) *The Orders of the National Curriculum*, London: HMSO.

Dillenbourg, P. (1999) *Collaborative Learning: Cognitive and Computational Approaches*, Oxford: Pergamon.

Dillenbourg, P., Baker, M., Blaye, A. and O'Malley, C. (1995) 'The evolution of research on collaborative learning', in H. Spada and P. Reiman (eds) *Learning in Humans and Machines: Towards an Interdisciplinary Learning Science*, Oxford: Elsevier.

Dillon, J.J. (ed.) (1988) *Questioning and Discussion: A Multidisciplinary Study*, London: Croom Helm.

Doise, W. and Mugny, G. (1984) *The Social Development of the Intellect*, Oxford: Pergamon Press.

Donaldson, M. (1978) *Children's Minds*, London: Fontana Press.

Edwards, D. and Mercer, N. (1987) *Common Knowledge: The Development of Understanding in the Classroom*, London: Methuen/Routledge.

Elbers, E. and Streefland, L. (2000) 'Collaborative learning and the construction of common knowledge', *European Journal of Psychology of Education* XV (4): 479–490.

Erickson, F. (1996) 'Going for the zone: the social and cognitive ecology of teacher–student interaction in classroom conversations', in D. Hicks (ed.) *Discourse, Learning and Schooling*, Cambridge: Cambridge University Press.

Fernández Cardenas, J.M. (2004) 'The appropriation and mastery of cultural tools in computer-supported collaborative literacy practices', doctoral thesis, Open University, Milton Keynes, UK.

Fernández, F., Wegerif, R., Mercer, N., Rojas-Drummond, S. (2001/2002) 'Reconceptualizing "scaffolding" and the Zone of Proximal Development in the context of symmetrical collaborative learning', *Journal of Classroom Interaction* 36/37 (2/1): 40–54.

Fisher, E. (1993) 'Distinctive features of pupil–pupil talk and their relationship to learning', *Language and Education* 7 (4): 239–258.

Fitzpatrick, H. (1996) 'Peer collaboration and the computer', unpublished doctoral thesis, University of Manchester.

Forman, E. (1996) 'Learning mathematics as participation in classroom practice: implications of sociocultural theory for educational reform', in L. Steffe, P. Nesher, P. Cobb, G. Goldin and B. Greer (eds) *Theories of Mathematical Learning*, Hillsdale, NJ: Erlbaum.

Fuchs, L.S. and Fuchs, D. (2000) 'Effects of workgroup structure and size on student productivity during collaborative work on complex tasks', *Elementary School Journal* 100 (3): 183.

Galton, M. and Williamson, J. (1992) *Group Work in the Primary Classroom*, London: Routledge.

Galton, M., Simon, B. and Croll, P. (1980) *Inside the Primary Classroom (the ORACLE Project)*, London: Routledge and Kegan Paul.

Galton, M., Hargreaves, L., Comber, C., Wall, D. and Pell, A. (1999) *Inside the Primary Classroom: 20 Years On*, London: Routledge.

Gee, J. (2000) 'Discourse and socio-cultural studies in reading', in M. Kamil, B. Mosenthal, P. Pearson and R. Barr (eds) *Handbook of Reading Research, Volume III*, London: Lawrence Erlbaum Associates.

Gee, J.P. (1999) *An Introduction to Discourse Analysis: Theory and Method*. London: Routledge.

Gee, J.P. (2003) *What Video Games Have to Teach us about Learning and Literacy*, London: Palgrave Macmillan.

Gee, J.P. (2004) *Situated Language and Learning: A Critique of Traditional Schooling*, London: Routledge.

Gee, J.P. and Green, J. (1998) 'Discourse analysis, learning and social practice: a methodological study', *Review of Research in Education* 23:119–169.

Gibbons, P. (2002) *Scaffolding Language, Scaffolding Learning: Teaching Second Language Learners in the Mainstream Classroom*, Portsmouth, NH: Heinemann.

Goldenberg, C. (1993) 'Instructional conversations: promoting comprehension through discussion', *The Reading Teacher* 46: 316–326.

Greenfield, P.M. and Lave, J. (1982) 'Cognitive aspects of informal education', in D. Wagner and H. Stephenson (eds) *Cultural Perspectives on Child Development*, San Francisco: Freeman.

Grice, H. (1975) 'Logic and conversation', in P. Cole and J. Morgan (eds) *Syntax and Semantics 3: Speech Acts*, New York: Academic Press.

Grossen, M. and Bachmann, K. (2000) 'Learning to collaborate in a peer-tutoring situation: who learns? what is learned?', *European Journal of Psychology of Education* XV (4): 491–508.

Halliday, M.A.K. (1978) *Language as a Social Semiotic: The Social Interpretation of Meaning*, London: Edward Arnold.

Halliday, M.A.K. and Hasan, R. (1976) *Cohesion in English*, London: Longman.

Hart, B. and Risley, T.R. (1995) *Meaningful Differences in the Everyday Experience of Young American Children*, New York: Brookes.

Hartup, W.W. (1998) 'The company they keep: friendships and their developmental significance', in A. Campbell and S. Muncer (eds) *The Social Child*, Hove: The Psychology Press.

Heath, S.B. (1983) *Ways with Words: Language, Life and Work in Communities and Classrooms*, Cambridge: Cambridge University Press.

Heritage, J. (1984) *Garfinkel and Ethnomethodology*, Cambridge: Polity Press.

Hester, S. and Francis, D. (2000) 'Ethnomethodology, conversational analysis and "institutional talk"', *Text* 20 (3): 391–413.

Hoogsteder, M., Maier, R. and Elbers, E. (1998) 'Adult–child interaction, joint problem solving and the structure of cooperation', in M. Woodhead, D. Faulkner and K. Littleton (eds) *Cultural Worlds of Early Childhood*, London: Routledge.

Howe, C. (1997) *Gender and Classroom Interaction: A Research Review*, Edinburgh: The Scottish Council for Research in Education.

Howe, C. and Tolmie, A. (1999) 'Productive interaction in the context of computer supported collaborative learning in science', in K. Littleton and P. Light (eds) *Learning with Computers: Analysing Productive Interaction*, London, Routledge.

Howes, C. and Ritchie, S. (2002) *A Matter of Trust: Connecting Teachers and Learners in the Early Childhood Classroom*, New York: Teachers College Press.

Issroff, K. (1999) 'Time-based analysis of students studying the Periodic Table', in K. Littleton and P. Light (eds) *Learning with Computers: Analysing Productive Interaction*, London: Routledge.

Järvelä, S. (1995) 'The cognitive apprenticeship model in a technologically rich learning environment: interpreting the learning interaction', *Learning and Instruction* 5 (3): 237–259.

Johnson, D.W. and Johnson, F. (1997) *Joining Together: Group Theory and Group Skills*, 6th edition, Boston: Allyn and Bacon.

Keefer, M., Zeitz, C. and Resnick, L. (2000) 'Judging the quality of peer-led student dialogues', *Cognition and Instruction* 18 (1): 53–81.

Keogh, T., Barnes, P., Joiner, R. and Littleton, K. (2000) 'Computers, verses, paper – girls versus boys: gender and task presentation effects', *Educational Psychology* 20 (1): 33–44.

Kim, I.-H., Anderson, R., Nguyen-Jahiel, K. and Archodidou, A. (in press) 'Discourse patterns during children's online discussions', *Journal of the Learning Sciences*.

Kleine-Staarman, J. (in press) 'Collaboration in CSCL: Social Interaction in Primary School Computer-Supported Collaborative Learning Environments', doctoral thesis submitted to Radboud University Nijmegen, The Netherlands, Institute of Behavioural Sciences.

Kumpulainen, K. and Wray, D. (eds) (2002) *Classroom Interaction and Social Learning: From Theory to Practice*, London: Routledge-Falmer.

Kutnick, P. (2005) 'Relational training for group working in classrooms: experimental and action research perspectives', paper presented as part of the *Educational Dialogue Research Unit Seminar Series*, Open University, Milton Keynes, June.

Kutnick, P. and Rogers, C. (1994) *Groups in Schools*, London: Cassell.

Lambirth, A. (2006) 'Challenging the laws of talk: ground rules, social reproduction and the curriculum', *The Curriculum Journal*, 17 (1): 59–71.

Lave, J. and Wenger, E. (1991) *Situated Learning: Legitimate Peripheral Participation*, Cambridge: Cambridge University Press.

Lemke, J. (2001) 'The long and the short of it: comments on multiple timescale studiers of human activity', *The Journal of the Learning Sciences* 10 (1 and 2): 17–26.

Light, P. (1997) 'Computers for learning: psychological perspectives', *Journal of Child Psychology and Psychiatry* 38 (5): 497–504.

Light, P. and Littleton, K. (1999) *Social Processes in Children's Learning*, Cambridge: Cambridge University Press.

Light, P., Sheldon, S. and Woodhead, M. (1991) *Learning to Think*, London: Routledge in association with the Open University.

Lipman, M. (1970) *Philosophy for Children*, Montclair, NJ: Institute for the Advancement of Philosophy for Children.

Littleton, K. (1999) 'Productivity through interaction: an overview', in K. Littleton and P. Light (eds) *Learning with Computers: Analyzing Productive Interaction*, London: Routledge.

Littleton, K. and Miell, D. (2004) 'Collaborative creativity: contemporary perspectives', in D. Miell and K. Littleton (eds) *Collaborative Creativity: Contemporary Perspectives*, London: Free Association Books.

Littleton, K. and Wood, C. (2006) 'Psychology and education: understanding teaching and learning', in C. Wood, K. Littleton and K. Sheehy (eds) *Developmental Psychology in Action*, Oxford: Blackwell Publishing.

Littleton, K., Miell, D. and Faulkner, D. (2004) *Learning to Collaborate, Collaborating to Learn*, New York: Nova Publishing.

Littleton, K., Mercer, N., Dawes, L., Wegerif, R., Rowe, D. and Sams, C. (2005) 'Thinking together at Key Stage 1', *Early Years: An International Journal of Research and Development* 25 (2): 165–180.

Makitalo, A. and Säljö, R. (2002) 'Talk in institutional context and institutional context in talk: categories as situated practices', *Text* 22 (1): 57–82.

Maybin, J. (2006) *Children's Voices: Talk, Knowledge and Identity*, Basingstoke: Palgrave Macmillan.

Maybin, J., Mercer, N. and Stierer, B. (1992) '"Scaffolding" learning in the classroom', in K. Norman (ed.) *Thinking Voices: The Work of the National Oracy Project*, London: Hodder and Stoughton.

Mercer, N. (1995) *The Guided Construction of Knowledge: Talk Amongst Teachers and Learners*, Clevedon: Multilingual Matters.

Mercer, N. (2000) *Words and Minds: How We Use Language to Think Together*, London: Routledge.

Mercer, N. (2005) 'Sociocultural discourse analysis: analysing classroom talk as a social mode of thinking', *Journal of Applied Linguistics* 1 (2): 137–168.

Mercer, N. and Sams, C. (2006) 'Teaching children how to use language to solve maths problems', *Language and Education* 20 (6): 507–527.

Mercer, N., Wegerif, R. and Dawes, L. (1999) 'Children's talk and the development of reasoning in the classroom', *British Educational Research Journal* 25 (1): 95–111.

Mercer, N., Littleton, K., Wegerif, R. (2004) 'Methods for studying the processes of interaction and collaborative activity in computer-based educational activities', *Technology, Pedagogy and Education*, 13 (2), 193–209.

Mercer, N., Dawes, R., Wegerif, R. and Sams, C. (2004) 'Reasoning as a scientist: ways of helping children to use language to learn science', *British Educational Research Journal* 30 (3): 367–385.

Michaels, S. and O'Connor, M.C. (2002) *Accountable Talk: Classroom Conversation That Works*, CD-ROM, Pittsburg, PA: University of Pittsburgh.

Miell, D. and Littleton, K. (eds) (2004) *Collaborative Creativity: Contemporary Perspectives*, London: Free Association Books.

Moll, L.C. (1990) 'Introduction', in L.C. Moll (ed.) *Vygotsky and Education: Instructional Implications and Applications of Sociohistorical Psychology*, Cambridge: Cambridge University Press.

Mortimer, E.F. and Scott, P.H. (2003) *Meaning Making in Science Classrooms*, Milton Keynes: Open University Press.

Mugny, G., Perret-Clermont, A-N. and Doise, W. (1981) 'Interpersonal co-ordinations and sociological differences in the construction of the intellect', in G. Stevenson and G. Davis (eds) *Applied Social Psychology*, Vol. 1, Chichester: Wiley.

Newman, D., Griffin, P. and Cole, M. (1989) *The Construction Zone: Working for Cognitive Change in School*, Cambridge: Cambridge University Press.

Norman, K. (ed.) (1992) *Thinking Voices: The Work of the National Oracy Project*, London: Hodder and Stoughton.

Nystrand, M. (1986) *The Structure of Written Communication: Studies of Reciprocity Between Writers and Readers*, London: Academic Press.

Nystrand, M., Wu, L., Gamorgan, A., Zeiser, S. and Long, D. (2003) 'Questions in time: investigating the structure and dynamics of unfolding classroom discourse', *Discourse Processes* 35 (2): 135–198.

Olson, D.R. (1994) *The World on Paper*, Cambridge: Cambridge University Press.

Papert, S. (1980) *Mindstorms: Children, Computers and Powerful Ideas*, New York: Basic Books.

Perret-Clermont, A-N. (1980) *Social Interaction and Cognitive Development in Children*, London: Academic Press.

Perret-Clermont, A-N. (1993) 'What is it that develops?' *Cognition and Instruction* 11 (3/4): 197–205.

Piaget, J. (1932) *The Moral Judgement of the Child*, London: Routledge.

Piaget, J. (1967) 'Development and learning', in E. Victor and M.S. Lerner (eds) *Readings in Science Education for the Elementary School*, New York: Macmillan.

Piaget, J. and Inhelder, B. (1956) *The Child's Conception of Space*, London: Routledge.

Rasmussen, I. (2005) 'Project work and ICT: studying learning as participation trajectories', Doctoral Thesis, Faculty of Education, University of Oslo: Norway.

Raven, J., Court, J. and Raven, J.C. (1995) *Manual For Raven's Progressive Matrices and Vocabulary Scales*, Oxford: Oxford Psychologists Press.

Resnick, L.B. (1999) 'Making America smarter', *Education Week Century Series* 18 (40): 38–40.

Resnick, L., Pontecorvo, C. and Säljö, R. (1997) 'Discourse, tools and reasoning', in L. Resnick, R. Säljö, C. Pontecorvo and B. Burge (eds) *Discourse, Tools and Reasoning: Essays on Situated Cognition*, Berlin and New York: Springer-Verlag.

Rogoff, B. (1990) *Apprenticeship in Thinking: Cognitive Development in Social Context*, Oxford: Oxford University Press.

Rojas-Drummond, S. (2000) 'Guided participation, discourse and the construction of knowledge in Mexican classroom', in H. Cowie and G. van der Aalsvoort (eds) *Social Interaction in Learning and Instruction*, Oxford: Pergamon.

Rojas-Drummond, S. and Mercer, N. (2004) 'Scaffolding the development of effective collaboration and learning', *International Journal of Educational Research* 39: 99–111.

Rojas-Drummond, S., Mercer, N. and Dabrowski, E. (2001) 'Collaboration, scaffolding and the promotion of problem solving strategies in Mexican pre-schoolers', *European Journal of Psychology of Education* XVI (2): 179–196.

Roth, W-M. (2001) 'Situating cognition', *The Journal of the Learning Sciences* 10 (1 and 2): 27–61.

Roth, W-M. (2005) *Talking Science: Language and Learning in Science*, Lanham, MD: Rowman and Littlefield.

Roth, W-M. (2006) *Learning Science: A Singular Plural Perspective*, Rotterdam: Sense Publishers.

Ryder, J. and Campbell, L. (1989) 'Groupsense: when groupwork does not add up to "groupwork"', *Pastoral Care in Education* 7 (1): 22–30.

Sams, C., Wegerif, R., Dawes, L. and Mercer, N. (2000) *Thinking Together with ICT and Primary Mathematics: A Continuing Professional Development Pack*, London: Smile Mathematics.

Schegloff, E. (1992) 'In another context', in A. Duranti and C. Goodwin (eds) *Rethinking Context: Language as an Interactive Phenomenon*, Cambridge: Cambridge University Press.

Schegloff, E. (1997) 'Whose text? Whose context?' *Discourse and Society*, 8 (2): 165–187.

Scott, P. (1998) 'Teacher talk and meaning making in science classrooms: a Vygotskian analysis and review', *Studies in Science Education* 32: 45–80.

Scott, P., Mortimer, E. and Aguiar, O. (2006) 'The tension between authoritative and dialogic discourse: a fundamental characteristic of meaning making interactions in high school science lessons', *Science Education* 90: 605–631.

Scott, P.H. and Asoko, H. (2006) 'Talk in science classrooms', in V. Wood-Robinson (ed.) *Association of Science Education Guide to Secondary Science Education*, Hatfield, Herts: Association for Science Education (ASE).

Sfard, A. and Kieran, C. (2001) 'Cognition as communication: rethinking learning-by-talking through multi-faceted analysis of students' mathematical interactions', *Mind, Culture, and Activity* 8 (1): 42–76.

Shayer, M. (2003) 'Not just Piaget; not just Vygotsky, and certainly not Vygotsky as alternative to Piaget', *Learning and Instruction* 13: 465–485.

Sinclair, J. and Coulthard, M. (1975) *Towards an Analysis of Discourse: The English Used by Teachers and Pupils*, Oxford: Oxford University Press.

Slavin, R.E. (1980) 'Co-operative learning', *Review of Educational Research* 50 (2): 315–342.

Swann, J. (1992) *Girls, Boys and Language*, London: Blackwell.

Tharp, R. and Gallimore, R. (1998) 'A theory of teaching as assisted performance', in D. Faulkner, K. Littleton and M. Woodhead (eds) *Learning Relationships in the Classroom*, London: Routledge.

Tharp, R.G. and Gallimore, R. (1988) *Rousing Minds to Life: Teaching, Learning and Schooling in Social Context*, Cambridge: Cambridge University Press.

The Open University (1991) *Talk and Learning 5–16: An In-Service Pack on Oracy for Teachers*, Milton Keynes: Open University.

Tudge, J. (1989) 'When collaboration leads to regression: some negative consequences of socio-cognitive conflict', *European Journal of Social Psychology* 19: 123–138.

Turkle, S. (1996) *Life on the Screen: Identity in the Age of Internet*, London: Weidenfeld and Nicholson.

Underwood, J. and Underwood, G. (1999) 'Task effects in co-operative and collaborative learning with computers', in K. Littleton, and P. Light (eds) *Learning with Computers: Analysing Productive Interaction*, London: Routledge.

Van Boxtel, C., Van der Linden, J. and Kanselaar, G. (2000) 'Collaborative learning tasks and the elaboration of conceptual knowledge', *Learning and Instruction*, 10 (4): 311–330.

Van Oers, B. and Hännikäinen, M. (2001) 'Some thoughts on togetherness: an introduction', *International Journal of Early Years Education* 9 (2): 101–108.

Vass, E. (2003) 'Understanding collaborative creativity: an observational study of the effects of the social and educational context on the processes of young children's joint creative writing', Doctoral Thesis, Milton Keynes: Open University.

Vygotsky, L.S. (1962) *Thought and Language*, Cambridge, MA: MIT Press

Vygotsky, L.S. (1978) *Mind in Society*, Cambridge, MA: Harvard University Press.

Vygotsky, L.S. (1981) 'The genesis of higher mental functions', in J.V. Wertsch (ed.) *The Concept of Activity in Soviet Psychology*, Armonk, NY: Sharpe.

Watkins, C. (2003) *Learning: A Sense Maker's Guide*, London: The Institute of Education.

Webb, N.M. (1989) 'Peer interaction and learning in small groups', *International Journal of Educational Research* 1 (1): 21–39.

Wegerif, R. (2004) 'The role of educational software as a support for teaching and learning conversations', *Computers and Education* 43: 179–191.

Wegerif, R. (in press (a)) 'From dialectic to dialogic: a response to Wertsch and Kazak', in T. Koschmann (ed.) *Theorizing Learning Practice*, Mahwah, NJ: Lawrence Erlbaum Associates.

Wegerif, R. (in press (b)) 'Dialogic or dialectic? The significance of ontological assumptions in research on educational dialogue', *British Educational Research Journal*.

Wegerif, R. and Dawes, L. (2004) *Thinking and Learning with ICT: Raising Achievement in Primary Classrooms*, London: Routledge.

Wegerif, R. and Mercer, N. (1997) 'Using computer-based text analysis to integrate qualitative and quantitative methods in the investigation of collaborative learning', *Language and Education* 11 (4): 271–286.

Wegerif, R. and Scrimshaw, P. (eds) (1997) *Computers and Talk in the Primary Classroom*, Clevedon: Multilingual Matters.

Wegerif, R., Littleton, K. and Jones, A. (2003) 'Stand-alone computers supporting learning dialogues in primary classrooms', *International Journal of Educational Research* 39 (8): 851–861.

Wegerif, R., Mercer, N. and Dawes, L. (1999) 'From social interaction to individual reasoning: an empirical investigation of a possible socio-cultural model of cognitive development', *Learning and Instruction* 9: 493–516.

Wells, G. (1986) *The Meaning Makers*, London: Hodder and Stoughton.

Wells, G. (1999) *Dialogic Enquiry: Toward a Sociocultural Practice and Theory of Education*, Cambridge: Cambridge University Press.

Wells, G. and Claxton, G. (eds) (2002) *Learning for Life in the 21st Century*, Oxford: Blackwell.

Wertsch, J. V. (ed.) (1985a) *Culture, Communication and Cognition: Vygotskian Perspectives*, Cambridge: Cambridge University Press.

Wertsch, J.V. (1985b) 'Adult–child interaction as a source of self-regulation in children', in S.R. Yussen (ed.) *The Growth of Reflection in Children*, Orlando, FL: Academic Press.

Wertsch, J. V. (1991a) 'A sociocultural approach to socially shared cognition', in L.B. Resnick, J.M. Levine, and S.D. Teasley (eds) *Perspectives on Socially Shared Cognition*, Washington: American Psychological Association.

Wertsch, J.V. (1991b) *Voices of the Mind: A Sociocultural Approach to Mediated Action*, London: Harvester Wheatsheaf.

Wertsch, J.V. (1997) 'The sociocultural approach to learning', paper presented to an Inaugural Conference of the Centre for Learning in Organisations, School of Education, University of Bristol, January.

Wilkinson, I. and Fung, I. (2002) 'Small group composition and peer effects', *International Journal of Educational Research* 37: 425–447.

Wood, D. (1992) 'Teaching talk', in K. Norman (ed.) *Thinking Voices: The Work of the National Oracy Project*, London: Hodder and Stoughton.

Wood, D. (1998) *How Children Think and Learn: The Social Contexts of Cognitive Development*, Oxford: Blackwell.

Wood, D. and Middleton, D. (1975) 'A study of assisted problem solving', *British Journal of Psychology* 66: 181–191.

Wood, D., Bruner, J. and Ross, G. (1976) 'The role of tutoring in problem solving', *Journal of Child Psychology and Psychiatry* 17: 89–100.

Wood, H., and Wood, D. (1999) 'Help seeking, learning and contingent tutoring', *Computers and Education* 33: 153–169.

Yackel, E., Cobb, P. and Wood, T. (1991) 'Small group interactions as a source of learning opportunities in second-grade mathematics', *Journal for Research in Mathematics Education* 22 (5): 390–408.

Youniss, J. (1999) 'Children's friendship and peer culture', in M. Woodhead, D. Faulkner and K. Littleton (eds) *Making Sense of Social Development*, London: Routledge.

Index